# WOMEN ENTREPRENEURS
# REWIRED TO RISE

### POWERFUL HABITS THAT BREAK THROUGH BURNOUT, SILENCE YOUR INNER CRITIC, AND BUILD A THRIVING BUSINESS FROM THE INSIDE OUT

**FIONA SOUTTER**

# © COPYRIGHT 2025 - ALL RIGHTS RESERVED.

The content contained within this book may not be reproduced, duplicated or transmitted without direct written permission from the author or the publisher.

Under no circumstances will any blame or legal responsibility be held against the publisher, or author, for any damages, reparation, or monetary loss due to the information contained within this book, either directly or indirectly.

**Legal Notice:**

This book is copyright protected. It is only for personal use. You cannot amend, distribute, sell, use, quote or paraphrase any part, or the content within this book, without the consent of the author or publisher.

**Disclaimer Notice:**

Please note the information contained within this document is for educational and entertainment purposes only. All effort has been executed to present accurate, up to date, reliable, complete information. No warranties of any kind are declared or implied. Readers acknowledge that the author is not engaged in the rendering of legal, financial, medical or professional advice. The content within this book has been derived from various sources. Please consult a licensed professional before attempting any techniques outlined in this book.

By reading this document, the reader agrees that under no circumstances is the author responsible for any losses, direct or indirect, that are incurred as a result of the use of the information contained within this document, including, but not limited to, errors, omissions, or inaccuracies.

ISBN: 978-1-7638713-4-2 (Paperback)

Published by Nexus Global Media

Email: contact@nexusglobal.media

*For those who illuminated my path—*
*To every spark of wisdom that ignited understanding,*
*Every guiding voice that spoke truth when I needed it most,*
*Every source of knowledge that transformed my journey.*
*Your guidance created ripples that*
*reached far beyond what you could see.*

*Each lesson, each insight, each moment of clarity*
*Has empowered not only my rise but fuels my deepest purpose:*
*To lift others as I have been lifted.*
*With profound gratitude for the light you've shared,*
*I dedicate this book to the beautiful cycle of*
*rising and raising others.*

*May these words continue the ripple effect—*
*From those who taught me,*
*Through me,*
*To you,*
*And beyond.*

*Fiona xx*

# CONTENTS

Introduction     vii

## PART ONE
## THE ROOT

1. The Energetic Essence of Being: Understanding Our Vibrational Nature     3
2. Understanding and Managing Your Vibrational State     11
3. Balancing Masculine and Feminine Energies for Peak Performance     19
4. Cultivating Joy as a Vibrational Strategy     29
5. The Power of Surrender: When Letting Go Becomes a Business Strategy     42
6. Energy Audit: What's Draining You, What's Fueling You, and What Needs to Change     53
7. Inner Child Healing for Aligned Business Growth     62
8. Unveiling Hidden Addictions That Hold You—and Your Business—Back     75
9. Reframing Your Language: The Words That Limit Your Results     83
10. The Mirror Principle: Your Business Reflects What You Believe About Yourself     90

Integration Point: Where Awareness Becomes Power     99
Make a Difference...     105

## PART TWO
## THE SHIFT

11. Morning Rituals for Centered, High-Frequency Workdays     109
12. Daily Practices Daily Practices that Anchor and Elevate You     119
13. Nourishing Your Mind: How Intentional Mental Input Shapes Your Business Output     129
14. Mindful Media Consumption: Curating Input to Protect Your Energy and Focus     136

| | |
|---|---|
| 15. From Body to Business: Physical Rituals That Fuel Vibrational Resilience | 145 |
| 16. Rhythms of Rest and Rejuvenation: Reclaiming Energy Through Cycles, Not Hustle | 156 |
| 17. Conscious Consumption That Supports Frequency, Focus, and Flow | 165 |
| 18. Creating Flow in Work and Life | 175 |
| Integration Point: Transitioning from Shift to Rise | 181 |

## PART THREE
## THE RISE

| | |
|---|---|
| 19. Becoming the Woman Who Rises: Embracing Growth as a Way of Being | 185 |
| 20. The Art of Pivoting: Navigating Change with Grace, Purpose, and Power | 191 |
| 21. Finding Your People: Building a Community That Nourishes and Elevates You | 199 |
| 22. Leading from Love, Not Fear in Business and Life | 211 |
| 23. Leading from the Heart to Create Authentic Influence | 221 |
| 24. Feeling It First: How Soulpreneurs Manifest Business Results Through Emotional Alignment | 229 |
| 25. Intuitive Intelligence: Trusting the Inner Guidance That Builds Aligned Success | 236 |
| 26. Soul Legacy: Creating Impact That Echoes Beyond Your Lifetime | 245 |
| 27. The Soulpreneur's Path: Your New Blueprint for Living, Leading, and Rising | 254 |
| Final Reflection: You Are Ready | 263 |
| References & Citations | 265 |
| About the Author | 271 |
| Also by Fiona Soutter | 273 |

# INTRODUCTION

When I first launched my e-commerce business, I was fueled by hope, driven by dreams, and guided by vision.

Like so many women who take the leap into entrepreneurship, I felt called to create something meaningful.

Something that was mine.

But I didn't realize that those dreams were just the tip of the iceberg—mere glimpses of a deeper becoming waiting to unfold.

The journey through entrepreneurship was anything but easy.

As the business expanded beyond what I'd imagined, I encountered challenges I never saw coming.

It wasn't about strategies or sales—those were the easy parts.

What surfaced were the deeper layers:

Self-doubt whispered "impostor syndrome" in my ear. Emotional triggers appeared in pitch meetings. I feared visibility when it was time to "lean in". I felt pressure to always be achieving, performing, and proving my worth in rooms where I was often the only woman.

Like you, I'd spent years striving to meet expectations. Society's. Investors'. And especially my own.

I thought if I could just bootstrap harder, pitch better, and network more effectively, it would all click into place.

But behind the scenes of my "success story", I was burnt out. Disconnected from myself. Quietly sabotaging the very business I was working so hard to scale.

That's when it hit me:

The biggest blocks in my business weren't outside of me. They weren't about access to capital or market conditions. They were within.

It became clear that the growth of my business was less about what I was doing and more about who I was being.

So I asked myself a question that changed everything:

Who do I need to **become** to lead this business into its fullest expression—and still maintain work-life integration in the process?

This book is a reflection of that journey inward.

The path I took when I realized that I couldn't build something truly meaningful from a fractured sense of self.

I had to heal. I had to rewire the subconscious patterns that were keeping me stuck. I had to realign with my truth.

Because here's the reality of being a female entrepreneur:

We're not just building businesses.

We're unlearning generations of people-pleasing, perfectionism, and programmed invisibility.

We're disrupting industries in a world that still defines power through a masculine lens while creating space for families, relationships, and our well-being.

And often, we do it while carrying the belief that we have to work twice as hard to be taken half as seriously.

This book exists to disrupt that narrative.

It's not another hustle-hard handbook or a one-size-fits-all business model.

It's not about adding more networking events to your calendar or perfecting your elevator pitch.

It's about changing how you see yourself. How you speak to yourself. How you show up in your business and life.

## THE JOURNEY AHEAD

This book unfolds as a journey of change in three parts—each addressing a critical dimension of your evolution as a woman building a business on your terms.

## THE ROOT

We begin at the foundation—the subconscious patterns and emotional blocks quietly sabotaging your growth.

Here, you'll discover how to:

- Identify the hidden stories shaping your entrepreneurial journey.
- Release inherited patterns around money, visibility, and worth.
- Release impostor syndrome and anchor into unshakeable self-trust

- Reconnect with your authentic voice after years of people-pleasing.

This isn't about finding what's "wrong" with you.

It's about bringing light to the root systems operating beneath the surface so you can consciously choose which ones to nurture and which to release.

## THE SHIFT

Once we understand the roots, we begin the shift—turning awareness into empowered action.

In this section, you'll learn how to:

- Rewire your neural pathways for confidence and clarity.
- Harness your feminine energy as a business advantage.
- Create boundaries that honor both your ambition and well-being.
- Redefine your relationship with time, productivity, and rest.

This is where the inner work meets outer application—where subtle adjustments in your energy create tangible changes in your business results.

## THE RISE

The final section focuses on embodiment—stepping fully into your power as a visionary leader.

Here, you'll discover how to:

- Lead from an authentic presence rather than performative hustle.

- Trust your intuition as a strategic business advantage.
- Create a legacy that reflects your deepest values.
- Become the Soulpreneur you were born to be.

This isn't about reaching a destination. It's about embracing a new way of being as you continue to evolve.

---

Inside each section, you'll find powerful practices—tools that have helped me break through self-sabotage, rewire my mindset around funding and growth, reconnect with my energy instead of burning out, and build a business that feels aligned with who I truly am.

Some come from mentors who understood my unique challenges as a woman in business. Others come straight from the pages of my personal journal during pivotal moments.

This isn't a book to rush through. It's a mentor in your corner.

And as you implement these changes, the changes don't just happen in your bottom line.

They ripple into your relationships. Your leadership style. Your capacity to create boundaries that honor both your ambition and well-being.

Launching and growing my business became the most catalytic vehicle for evolution I've ever known.

The woman who confidently walks into investor meetings today vastly differs from the one who began.

Through this journey, I came home to myself. I met the part of me that no longer needs to justify her place at the table. She simply leads from within.

And now, it's your turn.

My hope is that this book meets you wherever you are on your path—in the doubt about your next pivot, the overwhelm of scaling, the excitement of a new venture, or the deep knowing that you're ready to build something that reflects your true worth.

This is the work. This is the rise.

And I'll be walking it beside you, every step of the way.

Let's begin...

# PART ONE
# THE ROOT

## CHAPTER 1
# THE ENERGETIC ESSENCE OF BEING: UNDERSTANDING OUR VIBRATIONAL NATURE

YOU'VE FELT IT BEFORE, haven't you?

Someone walks into the room, and the whole atmosphere changes. You don't know why—but suddenly, everything feels lighter... or heavier. They haven't said a word. But their presence says everything.

We talk about people having "a good vibe." We say we feel drained around someone. Or that a space "just doesn't feel right."

These aren't throwaway observations. They're truth.

You're already sensing energy—every day. It's happening even if you've never been taught what to call it or how to work with it.

So if you're nodding your head right now, if you've ever felt something you couldn't quite explain but *knew* it was real—then you're already in touch with what this chapter is about. You don't need a degree in quantum physics to know that energy is real. Your body knows. Your intuition knows.

And now, it's time to consciously connect that knowing to who you are—and how you lead.

## ENERGY AS A TURNING POINT

I didn't always think about energy this way. Not consciously, at least.

After a car accident in 2014, everything changed. For an extended period of time, I was grappling with chronic pain—and when a series of difficult personal events collided—I was pulled into one of the darkest emotional periods I had ever faced.

The tools I'd relied on to keep moving—pushing through, staying positive, performing strength—just stopped working. I was stuck in a way I had never felt before. It wasn't just emotional. It was energetic.

I couldn't fake my way into feeling better. I couldn't hustle my way into happiness. I was finally face-to-face with something deeper: **my frequency**.

And it was in that place—deep in a pit of depression and anxiety—that I stumbled across something that reframed everything: *Dr. David Hawkins' Map of Consciousness.*

If you haven't seen it before, it's a chart that assigns **measurable vibrational frequencies to human emotions and states of being**. At the bottom of the scale are shame (20 Hz), guilt (30 Hz), grief (75 Hz), fear (100 Hz), and anger (150 Hz)—emotions that vibrate at the lowest frequencies. Further up the scale are emotions like courage (200 Hz), neutrality, acceptance (350 Hz), and eventually, joy (540 Hz), love (500 Hz), and peace (600 Hz).

When I first saw it, something cracked open in me.

I realized that while I was *currently* living in those lower vibrational states... I had actually been *carrying* many of those emotions for most of my life. I'd just become good at masking them. Suppressing them. Outperforming them.

And even more than that, I began to understand that my emotional state wasn't just about how I felt.

It was shaping how I lived. It was influencing what I attracted. It was forming the energetic foundation of my entire reality.

That discovery opened the door to everything that came next.

Soon after, I picked up Michael Singer's *The Untethered Soul*, a book that helped me explore the connection between our inner world and the energy that moves through it even more deeply.

> *"The foundations of spiritual growth and personal awakening are very much strengthened by the findings of Western science. Science has shown us how an underlying energy field forms into atoms, which then bind together into molecules and ultimately manifest into the entire physical universe. The same is true inside of us... Regardless of what you call this inner force—chi, Shakti, or spirit—it is an underlying energy that flows in particular patterns through your inner being."*
>
> — Michael Singer

Reading those words was like flipping on a light switch.

It made me realize something I'd never been taught—not in school, not in business, and certainly not in the traditional personal development space:

We are energy.

Not in a poetic, "good vibes only" way. In a literal, measurable, scientific way.

📚 **Explore More**

Want to deepen your understanding of vibrational states? Search online for **Dr. David Hawkins' Map of Consciousness**—a visual chart that links emotional states to measurable frequencies. Reflect on where you've been operating from and where you want to lead from now.

---

## THE SCIENCE OF OUR ENERGETIC NATURE

You might've heard it said that we're 99.9999999% empty space. That's not just spiritual language—that's quantum physics. When you break us down to the atomic level—beyond cells, beyond molecules—we are mostly space. And that space?

It's energy in motion.

Vibrating.
Responding.
Interacting with everything.

So what looks solid—your body, your environment, even this sentence on the page—is actually made up of frequency.

We aren't just having experiences. We're emitting energy all the time, and that energy is affecting everything.

Your emotional state isn't just a passing mood. It's a frequency that radiates outward.

Your thoughts aren't just mental chatter. They're signals that influence your biology, your behaviour, and your reality.

Dr. Joe Dispenza, a world-renowned neuroscientist and bestselling author known for his research on neuroplasticity and mind-body healing, opened up a whole new level of understanding for me. His research shows that our thoughts and emotions emit measurable electromagnetic frequencies that influence how we feel and how our bodies function. When we chance our internal state, we change our energetic signature—and with that, we change what we attract and experience.

Then, I came across Dr. Bruce Lipton's work on epigenetics, which blew my mind. His research shows that our thoughts and beliefs can affect gene expression, meaning we're not victims of our biology but participants in it. Our energy—through our emotions, perceptions, and inner narratives—shapes us on a cellular level.

And then there's Nikola Tesla, who famously said:

> "If you want to find the secrets of the universe, think in terms of energy, frequency, and vibration."

Tesla wasn't being poetic. He was telling us how reality works.

Everything in the universe—including you—is made up of energy vibrating at specific frequencies. Your body. Your thoughts. Your emotions. But here's what most business books don't tell you:

Your business itself is energy. Your client relationships are energy. And yes, money is pure energy.

Think about it. Money isn't really paper or digital numbers—it's a representation of value exchanged, it's flow, it's agreement. It's energy in motion. When money feels "stuck" in your business, that's not just a cash flow problem—it's an energetic blockage.

According to the Law of Resonance—a principle rooted in quantum physics—the energy you emit doesn't stay inside you. It interacts with everything around you. Your business included.

Like attracts like.

Your emotional state becomes your energetic signature. Your thoughts and beliefs act like tuning forks, attracting clients, opportunities, and circumstances that match your current frequency.

When we understand this, entrepreneurship becomes something entirely different. It's no longer just about strategy, marketing funnels, and Instagram posts. It becomes a conscious practice of energy management.

Because the truth is, your business can only grow to the extent that your energy allows it to.

## 🌀 TRY THIS: FEEL YOUR FREQUENCY

Pause for 60 seconds right now. Close your eyes. Take a few slow, conscious breaths. Then ask yourself:

- *What does my energy feel like right now?*
- *Is it light or heavy?*
- *Calm or chaotic?*
- *Expansive or tight?*

No need to fix it. Just witness it. This simple act of observation is an energetic reset—and the first step to creating from alignment.

## ENERGY ISN'T WOO WOO—IT'S PHYSICS

In a world obsessed with performance and productivity—especially in business and entrepreneurship—starting with energy might seem unconventional.

After all, we're usually taught that success comes from action, strategy, and output. But most people miss the point: strategy can only take you as far as your state allows.

This book isn't about discarding logic. It's about understanding that your energy is the *lens* through which every decision, every launch, and every conversation flows.

Without energetic alignment, even the best plan falls flat. But when your frequency aligns with your vision, everything begins to move with you.

Business isn't just built by what you do. It's shaped by the energy you bring to what you do.

And that's not woo woo. It's physics.

## EMBODYING ENERGY AS FEMININE POWER

As women, we have a unique relationship with energy. Our cycles, our emotions, our instincts—all of it is rich with wisdom. And yet, we've been taught to see these things as inconvenient or weak.

But when we begin to understand ourselves as energetic beings, we reclaim those parts. We stop seeing sensitivity as a liability and start seeing it as data. We begin to honour rhythm instead of resisting it. We lead from presence instead of pressure.

This isn't just conceptual—it's biological.

Women tend to have a thicker corpus callosum (the bridge between the left and right brain), allowing better integration of logic and emotion—a key factor in intuitive processing. Our hormonal rhythms create natural windows of introspection, heightened sensitivity, and energetic awareness. These energetic fluctuations refine our ability to detect micro-level emotional and behavioural patterns—internally and externally.

What has often been labeled as women being "too emotional" is actually an advanced capacity to perceive and respond to energy. Sensitivity isn't weakness—it's wisdom.

This idea of *energetic embodiment* is a cornerstone of feminine leadership—and it will weave through many of the practices you'll explore in the coming chapters. For now, simply notice how your relationship with your energy softens when you allow yourself to feel it rather than fight it.

## CLOSING REFLECTION

As we begin this journey together, I want you to remember this: your energy isn't a side note in your business—it's the foundation. The more you understand how your vibrational state influences your thoughts, confidence, health, and how the world responds to you, the more you reclaim your power.

You don't need to become someone else. You just need to return to the truth of who you already are—an energetic being, designed to feel, create, and lead from the inside out.

In the chapters ahead, we'll explore exactly how this energetic understanding reshapes your business decisions, leadership approach, and entrepreneurial journey.

Let's keep going. You're just getting started.

# CHAPTER 2
# UNDERSTANDING AND MANAGING YOUR VIBRATIONAL STATE

IF CHAPTER 1 helped you understand that you are an energetic being, then this chapter will show you what to do with that awareness.

Because once you accept that everything is energy—your thoughts, emotions, body, actions, and outcomes—the next question becomes: How do I manage my own vibrational state?

## WHAT IS A VIBRATIONAL STATE?

Your vibrational state is the total of your frequency in any given moment, shaped by your emotions, thoughts, body language, energy field, and level of presence. It isn't just spiritual language. It's physics, biology, and emotion—all interwoven.

Think of it like a radio station. Whatever frequency you're tuned into is the signal you're broadcasting. And just like with a radio, what you tune into determines what you hear and attract.

We constantly communicate with the world through energy—not just through words or actions, but through how we show up.

And whether or not we realize it, that energy impacts everything: Our relationships. Our business. Our creativity. Our capacity to lead.

## THE SCIENCE OF VIBRATIONAL AWARENESS

As we explored in Chapter 1, Hawkins' *Map of Consciousness* provides a framework for understanding how our emotional states affect our frequency. His research confirms that higher vibrational states create expansiveness and connection, while lower frequencies lead to constriction and isolation in our physical and emotional experiences.

Other research supports this understanding:

- **Dr. Bruce Lipton's** work demonstrates how our thoughts and beliefs directly affect our biological processes and genetic expression.
- **Dr. Joe Dispenza's** research shows that elevating our emotional states brings about measurable changes in our physical health and quality of life.
- **The HeartMath Institute's** research demonstrates how heart coherence—a measurable state facilitated by positive emotional states—can improve cognitive functioning and emotional stability.

These scientific perspectives show that our emotional and energetic baseline affects our nervous system, hormones, immune system, and even gene expression.

This means managing your vibrational state is not just about "feeling good"—it's about regulating your nervous system, optimising your health, and becoming a clearer vessel for creative and aligned decision-making.

## WHY THIS AWARENESS MATTERS

When you know your energetic state—and take responsibility for it—you become the creator of your experience, not the reactor.

That doesn't mean forcing yourself into "high vibes only" or bypassing difficult feelings. It's about recognising your current state—and intentionally choosing a different one when it no longer serves you.

Some days, you'll feel clear, calm, and connected. Other days, you'll feel stuck, overwhelmed, or reactive.

The difference isn't in how you feel—it's in what you do with that awareness.

People naturally respond to vibrational states, often without conscious realization. We've all encountered someone who seems to positively affect the energy of an entire room, or conversely, someone whose presence creates immediate discomfort or tension. This intuitive ability to sense energy stems from our biological and psychological mechanisms that detect and react to subtle environmental cues.

## BECOMING THE WITNESS

One of the most impactful practices I've learned—and continue to use daily—is what I call **becoming the witness**.

It means stepping back and observing your internal state without judgment.

Noticing the thoughts.
Noticing the emotion.
Noticing the energy... and simply witnessing it.

No fixing. No bypassing. Just allowing.

This simple act of presence creates space.

And in that space, you reclaim your power.

You don't have to change your state instantly—in fact, trying to force it usually pulls you deeper into resistance. But when you simply observe what's there without attaching to it, you often shift naturally.

This practice has changed everything for me—especially in business, where emotional triggers used to run the show.

I remember preparing for a high-stakes pitch meeting while feeling completely off.

My energy was scattered. My confidence was shaky. That old *"Who am I to ask for this kind of investment?"* story was on repeat.

The old me would have masked it. Forced a power stance. Pushed through the fear with fake confidence and adrenaline. Instead, that day, I did something different.

I took ten quiet minutes. I sat down. I became the witness.

I acknowledged the impostor syndrome. I felt the nervous flutter in my solar plexus. I breathed with it—not to escape it, but to *be* with it.

And as I observed the pattern, I asked myself a simple but powerful question:

*"Does this story serve my higher self?"*

When I answered honestly, I saw the truth: it didn't.

It was just a program—an old story I had outgrown.

And because I could see it clearly, I could also **release it**.

No drama. No internal war. Just... *let go...*

The presentation that followed wasn't compelling just because of the slides or strategy—it landed because I was **energetically congruent**. The investors felt it. They trusted it. And they said yes.

That wasn't a coincidence.

That was **vibration in action**.

And that's the power of witnessing: When you create space between you and your inner noise, your true self begins to lead.

## THE INVISIBLE IMPACT OF YOUR STATE

If you're leading a team, writing copy, holding a sales call, recording a video, or simply making a decision, your energy is speaking louder than your words.

Clients can feel it. Your audience can feel it. Even your tech, your timing, your traction—they often mirror your internal state.

When you're clear, calm, and congruent—your communication lands. When you're desperate, chaotic, or in lack, even the most "perfect" strategy falls flat.

This isn't magic. It's **frequency**.

And it's why managing your energetic state becomes one of the most game-changing leadership practices you'll ever develop.

## VIBRATIONAL STATES IN BUSINESS CONTEXTS

How your energetic state affects specific business activities:

- **Client Interactions:** When you vibrate at a frequency of service and are certain of your value, potential clients naturally lean in.

- **Content Creation:** When you create from alignment and genuine desire to serve, your message resonates in a way that algorithm-chasing never will.

- **Decision-Making:** The same decision made from a state of trust unfolds naturally, often leading to opportunities you couldn't have planned for.

- **Team Leadership:** Your team doesn't just respond to what you say—they attune to how you feel. Your vibrational state sets the tone for your entire organization.

- **Money Mindset:** The subtle difference between "I hope they can afford me" and "This is the investment for the deep personal growth I provide" directly impacts your revenue, client quality, and the ease with which money flows to you.

## GENTLE NOTE ON TRAUMA & ENERGY BLOCKS

It's important to acknowledge that low vibrational states aren't always about bad habits or surface-level negativity. Often, they're connected to unresolved trauma, suppressed emotions, and old programming that was installed long before we had the tools to process it.

These stored patterns can unconsciously affect our energy field, keeping us anchored in fear, shame, guilt, or over-control—even when our conscious mind is saying we want something different.

In later chapters, we'll explore emotional healing, boundaries, self-love, and inner child work more deeply.

But for now, just know this:

Your vibrational state isn't fixed. And what you feel isn't who you are. It's just what you've learned to carry—and what you now have the power to release.

## ⊙ TRY THIS:

**Daily Energetic Check-In**

Take 2-3 minutes each day to ask:

*What am I feeling right now?*
*What's the energy behind it?*
*What's one thing I could do—or stop doing—to soften into a higher state?*

Write it down if it helps. Breathe into it. And remember—the goal isn't perfection. It's presence.

**Pattern Interrupt Practice**

When you notice yourself in a lower vibrational state during your workday:

1. Pause and physically change your environment (step outside, move to a different room)
2. Place one hand on your heart, one on your belly
3. Take 3 deep breaths, imagining light entering with each inhale
4. Ask: "What would serve my highest good in this moment?"
5. Take one aligned action based on your answer

This 60-second reset can change your state before important calls, difficult conversations, or creative blocks.

## CLOSING REFLECTION: FROM AWARENESS TO INTEGRATION

As we close this chapter, I invite you to practice noticing your vibrational state throughout your day. This isn't about judgment or forcing yourself to "be positive"—it's about *developing the awareness that precedes genuine meaningful change.*

Remember that this journey isn't linear. There will be days when you feel completely aligned and others when old patterns seem to take over. It's not about how quickly you recalibrate—it's about your commitment to meet each moment with compassion.

Throughout the rest of this book, we'll explore multiple ways to raise your vibrational state— from balancing masculine and feminine energies in Chapter 3, to cultivating joy in Chapter 4, embracing laughter in Chapter 5, and practicing surrender in Chapter 6. Each of these practices offers a unique pathway to elevating your frequency and a more empowered entrepreneurial journey.

For now, simply practice becoming the witness of your energy. Notice how it fluctuates. Observe how it affects your business decisions, your creative output, and your leadership presence.

And remember—your vibrational state is a practice, not a destination. Each moment offers a new opportunity to choose your frequency.

# CHAPTER 3
# BALANCING MASCULINE AND FEMININE ENERGIES FOR PEAK PERFORMANCE

FOR MOST OF MY LIFE, I was in "go-go-go" mode.

Even as a young girl, I learned how to take care of things myself. I had to.

There were valid reasons for it—and I now understand it wasn't just about independence or drive.

It was my nervous system.

I was operating in a chronic state of fight or flight.

Always alert.
Always anticipating.
Always doing.

And the world rewarded it.

Especially in business.

It wasn't until years later—well into my entrepreneurial journey—that I realized I had been stuck in this hyper-masculine way of being.

Not because I'm masculine by nature but because I had been surviving that way for so long that I didn't know anything different.

Rest made me uncomfortable.
Receiving felt indulgent.
Softness felt unsafe.

Every time I tried to honour the feminine energy parts of myself—the parts that needed stillness, flow, or gentleness—guilt would rise like a wave.

It whispered things like:

*You're being lazy.*
*You're not doing enough.*
*You're falling behind.*

So I'd override the message. Push through. Prove my worth through output.

Sound familiar?

So many women—especially those with ambition, big hearts, and big visions—find themselves stuck in this loop. And it's not our fault. We've been conditioned to equate value with performance. And in the business world, where structure, strategy, logic, and linearity dominate, it's easy to lose touch with the softer side of our power.

But here's what I want you to know:

You were never meant to build your business from burnout.

You were meant to **build from balance**.

And that starts with understanding the two energies at play within you—the masculine and the feminine—and how integrating them can lead to true, sustainable, soul-aligned success.

## THE ENERGETIC DUALITY WITHIN

You hold both masculine and feminine energy within you.

We all do.

This isn't about gender or identity—it's about the two energetic forces that move through everything in life and business. When they're in harmony, we feel grounded, clear, and strong. When they're out of balance, we feel stuck, depleted, or disconnected from ourselves.

So what are these energies?

Masculine energy is the part of you that's focused, structured, goal-oriented, and decisive. It's the planner. The builder. The one that gets things done. It's linear, purpose-driven, and thrives on direction, logic, and progress.

Feminine energy, on the other hand, is the part of you that flows, feels, creates, and receives. It's intuitive, emotional, magnetic. It lives in your body, your senses, and your ability to be present. It doesn't need a straight line—it moves in rhythm and response.

Neither energy is better than the other.

And true power doesn't come from choosing one—it comes from integrating both.

The masculine provides the container. The feminine fills it with life.

One is the riverbank. The other is the water.

When they work together, your energy becomes clear, coherent, and deeply magnetic.

## THE ORIGINS OF MASCULINE & FEMININE ENERGY CONCEPTS

You might wonder: Why do we label certain qualities as "masculine" or "feminine"? These concepts have deep historical and cross-cultural roots that transcend modern understanding.

Ancient traditions worldwide recognized these complementary energies:

- In Chinese philosophy: Yin (feminine) and Yang (masculine)
- In Hinduism: Shiva (masculine consciousness) and Shakti (feminine creative power)
- Indigenous wisdom speaks of Father Sky (masculine) and Mother Earth (feminine)
- Carl Jung explored these as anima (feminine aspect in men) and animus (masculine aspect in women)

What's fascinating is the remarkable consistency across different cultures in which qualities are associated with each energy. This suggests we're tapping into fundamental forces that transcend gender roles.

In modern business contexts, we've inherited systems that heavily favor masculine energy qualities. By understanding these concepts, we're not reinforcing stereotypes—we're challenging the system that says only one type of energy is valuable in leadership and success.

See Table 3.1 for a quick comparison of the different qualities associated with masculine and feminine energies.

## TABLE 3.1 RECOGNIZING THE ENERGIES

| Masculine Energy | Feminine Energy |
|---|---|
| Linear, structured | Cyclical, flowing |
| Goal-oriented | Process-oriented |
| Action-focused | Receptivity-focused |
| Doing | Being |
| Strategic planning | Intuitive knowing |
| External metrics | Internal feeling states |
| Protection | Creation |
| Direction | Expansion |

## ! WHEN WE'RE OUT OF BALANCE

When we're out of balance, we feel it.

Maybe not right away. Maybe not all at once. But eventually, the symptoms start showing up.

Too much masculine energy—without the balance of the feminine—often looks like:

- Chronic overthinking and over planning
- Hustling without pause
- Struggling to rest, even when exhausted
- Needing to control every detail
- Equating worth with productivity
- Leading with logic while ignoring intuition

And let's be real—in the world of entrepreneurship, this is the most common imbalance for women.

We've been taught that success comes from pushing, striving, and doing more. And when we operate in that masculine mode for too long, we burn out. We disconnect from our bodies. We start ignoring the signals that tell us when something's off—and we stop trusting ourselves.

True power lives in both.

In knowing when to lead from your masculine and when to soften into your feminine.

Knowing how to move between structure and flow, strategy and intuition, action and rest—without guilt or fear—is key.

This isn't about balancing your calendar.

It's about balancing your energy.

## WHY THIS IS SO COMMON FOR WOMEN ENTREPRENEURS?

There's a reason so many women in business feel disconnected from their feminine energy—or unsure how to access it without guilt.

The business world was built on masculine foundations: strategy, logic, speed, control, and hierarchy.

And while those qualities absolutely have value, the system itself often leaves no space for intuition, emotion, softness, or rest.

We've been taught—consciously or not—that those qualities are weaknesses. To be taken seriously in leadership or entrepreneurship, we have to toughen up, push through, and keep proving.

So what do we do?

We lean harder into our masculine energy. We overperform. We overgive. We override. And slowly, we lose access to the parts of ourselves that actually make us magnetic, creative, and deeply wise.

It's not that we lack feminine energy; it's that we've been taught not to trust it.

Because feminine energy doesn't always follow a plan. It doesn't thrive in a rush. It doesn't push. It listens.

It moves through the body. It speaks in sensation. It works in cycles, not deadlines.

Unless we've learned how to honour that part of ourselves without judgment, we're likely to default to masculine patterns of leadership that leave us feeling drained, disconnected, or misaligned.

## THE SCIENCE BEHIND THE BALANCE

This isn't just conceptual—there's a neurobiological component too. The constant "doing" mode activates our sympathetic nervous system (fight-or-flight), while the "being" mode engages our parasympathetic system (rest-and-digest). We literally need both for optimal brain function and creativity.

When we stay locked in sympathetic dominance—always in that masculine energy of pushing and doing—our bodies produce higher levels of cortisol and adrenaline. Over time, this impacts everything from our immune function to our decision-making abilities.

Balance isn't just about feeling better. It's about optimizing your biological systems for peak performance.

## REAL RESULTS: BEYOND THEORY

One client came to me operating entirely from masculine energy—

14-hour workdays, rigid systems, and constant hustle. Her business was growing, but she was drowning.

Within three months of rebalancing her energies—adding intuitive decision-making and scheduled rest periods—her conversion rate increased by 20%. But more importantly, she stopped dreading her business.

That's the power of energetic coherence.

When your energies are balanced, you notice tangible shifts:

- Your content resonates more deeply
- Your offers align naturally with client needs
- Your marketing feels authentic rather than forced
- Your energy isn't depleted after client calls
- Your pricing decisions come from worth, not fear

These translate directly to client retention, conversion rates, and sustainable revenue.

## REBALANCING FROM WITHIN

So, how do we begin returning to balance?

Not by swinging to the opposite extreme and not by rejecting the structure or discipline that has likely served us in parts of our journey. The path to energetic harmony isn't found in abandoning the masculine but in integrating it with the often-overlooked wisdom of the feminine.

It begins with noticing.

Noticing when we're in overdrive, when we override our own needs, or when we find ourselves performing from strength rather than embodying grounded power. These moments of recognition don't require immediate change—they simply invite awareness. And awareness is the starting point for everything.

From that place, we begin making subtle, conscious choices. Maybe that means pausing between meetings instead of rushing. Perhaps it's choosing rest without guilt. It might be listening to the quiet nudge that says this isn't right—and trusting that voice instead of dismissing it.

Rebalancing doesn't require a dramatic overhaul of your life. Often, it's a series of micro-adjustments made with compassion. You begin building your business not just with structure and strategy but also with softness, spaciousness, and intuition.

---

## 🌀 TRY THIS

**Energy Pulse Check**

Take a moment to reflect: Are you currently leaning more into *doing* or *being*?

Is that what's truly needed in this moment, or are you responding out of habit, fear, or pressure?

There's no wrong answer. Just awareness.

As you move through the week, keep asking yourself this question and notice how your energy gently realigns

**The 60-Second Reset**

When you notice yourself stuck in overdrive:

- Place one hand on your heart, one on your belly.

- Take three deep breaths, extending the exhale.
- Ask: *"What would feel supportive right now?"*
- Listen to the first answer that arises.

This simple practice helps shift you from doing to sensing—from masculine to feminine energy—in under a minute.

---

## CLOSING REFLECTION

This isn't about finding a perfect balance. Life is rarely that clean. Some seasons require more output, more structure, more fire. Others call for stillness, softness, and slowing down. The point isn't to live equally in both energies at all times—it's to lead with awareness of what's needed and permission to honour both.

You are allowed to lead with strength and softness.

To be powerful and receptive.

To build systems and honour your cycles.

Peak performance doesn't come from constant striving. It comes from energetic harmony—with yourself, your season, your truth.

And that harmony begins when you remember that you are both.

# CHAPTER 4
# CULTIVATING JOY AS A VIBRATIONAL STRATEGY

NOT LONG AGO, I was walking on the beach when I ran into my neighbor. We started chatting, and he confided in me. His shoulders slumped slightly as he described feeling a persistent emptiness —like something vital was missing from his life—though he couldn't quite identify what it was.

I looked at him and gently asked,

"When was the last time you remember feeling joy?"

He paused. Really paused. Then said,

"I honestly don't know."

I could feel the weight of that answer.

Not just in him—but in me.

Still, I thought maybe if I could help him remember, it might spark something. So I followed up:

"Okay... what kind of things bring you joy?"

Again, he paused. This time even longer. He looked at me and said,

"I can't think of anything. I don't know."

That moment landed in my chest like a stone—not because I was shocked, but because I've been there, too.

I remember seasons in my life when joy felt so far away that I wouldn't have known how to describe it, let alone access it. When every day felt like a repeat of the last—wake up, work, eat, sleep. On the surface, everything looked "fine." But underneath, I felt flat. Disconnected. Dull.

I wasn't sad. I was disconnected from joy—and I didn't even realize how much that mattered.

The reality is, many women feel this way—especially high-achieving women who are holding businesses, teams, families, households, and dreams together.

Joy starts to feel like a luxury.

Something you'll get to... after the to-do list is done.

But the to-do list is never done. And the joy keeps getting pushed further and further away.

Here's what I want you to hear:

Joy isn't just a "nice to have." It's a vibrational strategy.

On Hawkins' scale of consciousness, joy ranks even higher than love. It's expansive. Regenerative. Potent.

When you elevate your vibrational state through joy, you literally change the energy you bring to every aspect of your business—from the content you create to the clients you attract to the revenue you generate.

So, no, joy isn't frivolous.

It's fuel.

## UNDERSTANDING JOY VS. HAPPINESS

It's worth saying here—joy is not the same as happiness.

Happiness is often a response to something external. A kind word. A sunny day. A fresh cup of coffee. It feels good—light, bright, and often fleeting. It's what we feel when something outside of us gives us a reason to smile.

Joy is different.
Joy runs deeper.
Joy doesn't need a reason.

It's a state of being—a sense of inner coherence that lives in the body, not just the mind. It can feel like ease, presence, or quiet gratitude. It can show up in soft moments, not just in celebration.

Think of it this way:

The coffee might make you happy, but the joy comes from fully experiencing the warmth spreading through your hands, the aroma filling your senses, and the moment of presence as you pause your busy day. The coffee is external—the joy is in your relationship with that moment.

You can feel happiness without joy, but it often feels a little empty—like you're smiling, but not lit up from within.

Joy has fullness to it.
Rootedness.
Wholeness.

It's not about feeling good all the time—it's about feeling connected to yourself, to your aliveness, to the present moment.

And once you learn to recognise joy, even in the smallest flickers, you can begin to choose it more often.

Not wait for it.
Not earn it.
But invite it in—because it's always available.

## THE SCIENCE OF JOY

When we talk about joy, we're not just speaking metaphorically. There's real science behind how this state impacts our biology and energy.

Psychologist Barbara Fredrickson's research has shown that joy—and other high-frequency emotions—actually broaden our perception and make us more open to new ideas and creative solutions. In other words, joy opens the mind (Fredrickson, 2001).

Even the smallest flicker of joy can ripple out into how we think, feel, relate, and respond. It draws our awareness into the present, helping us notice what's good, what's beautiful, and what's already working.

And when joy expresses itself as laughter, the physiological benefits multiply:

- Endorphins ease pain and elevate mood
- Dopamine boosts motivation and creative risk-taking
- Serotonin improves emotional regulation

Simultaneously, laughter reduces cortisol (the stress hormone), lowers blood pressure, and enhances cognitive flexibility.

From a vibrational standpoint, **joy is a direct frequency elevator**. It shakes off density, clears emotional stagnation, and invites expansion. It gets energy moving—fast.

This isn't just feeling better. This is actually operating at a higher frequency.

## WHY JOY CAN FEEL HARD TO ACCESS

If you're someone who is finding it hard to feel joy, you're not alone.

I've witnessed it time and again—in coaching conversations, casual chats, and even in my own reflection. Somewhere along the way, many of us disconnected from joy—not because we wanted to—but because life got heavy. Fast.

We enter what many call "Groundhog Day" living—the routine of waking up, working, caring for others, eating, sleeping, and repeating. Our days are packed, our nervous systems are overstimulated, and our minds are chasing to-do lists we never seem to finish. And before we know it, we're functioning—but we're not feeling.

Joy becomes something we vaguely remember but rarely experience. Or worse, we start believing it's something we have to earn.

And here's the deeper truth:

Many women—especially those of us wired to achieve—have been conditioned out of joy. We were raised in systems that praised productivity over presence and self-sacrifice over self-connection. We learned to value what we do, not how we feel.

For some, joy was never modelled. For others, it was discouraged.

Be serious.
Focus.
Stop daydreaming.
Don't be too loud.
Don't be too much.

And if we grew up in environments where joy felt unsafe or inconsistent, our nervous systems may have unconsciously learned to associate joy with risk. In those cases, our bodies began to feel more "at home" in stress than in lightness—not because joy is bad, but because safety was tied to vigilance.

This doesn't mean you're broken. It means your body got really good at protecting you.

But that protection came at a cost: your connection to joy, aliveness, and the ability to express that joy through laughter.

If joy feels distant, you're not doing it wrong. It's not lost. It's simply waiting for you to come back to it—gently, without pressure, and without guilt.

## RECONNECTING WITH JOY

Joy isn't something you wait for. It's something you return to—one small moment at a time.

And often, when you've been disconnected from it for a long time, it's not the big moments that help you reconnect. It's the quiet ones:

- The sunlight streaming through your window
- The smell of your favorite candle
- A long exhale you didn't know you needed
- That feeling of peace after a hard cry

Joy isn't always loud or ecstatic. Sometimes it's soft. Sacred. Subtle. And sometimes, it's so quiet you have to slow down just to hear it.

If joy feels far away, begin by asking yourself:

- When do I feel most like myself?
- What used to make me smile—before life got so busy?

- What's one small thing that brings me lightness, even for a moment?

Then start looking for those moments. Noticing them. Naming them. Because what we name, we claim. And what we pay attention to expands.

---

## 🌀 TRY THIS: MICRO-MOMENTS OF JOY

At the end of today, jot down three small moments when you felt even a flicker of joy—even if it was fleeting.

The warmth spreading through your hands as you hold a cup of tea. The aliveness in your body when you let yourself move to a song you love. The openness in your chest as you take a deep breath of fresh air.

Don't judge the moment. Just notice it. Let it be enough.

Over time, this practice rewires your brain—and your frequency—to begin recognizing joy more naturally.

---

## LAUGHTER: JOY'S PUREST EXPRESSION

There's a moment—right after a deep, genuine laugh—when everything softens.

Your body relaxes.
Your shoulders drop.
Your breath deepens.
Your whole nervous system exhales.

That's not just emotion. That's joy manifesting in its most beautiful form.

Laughter is one of joy's purest expressions—emerging from deep within the soul. It opens a window in even the heaviest room. It breaks the tension. It changes the vibration of everything around it —and within it.

And yet, as adults—and especially as women in business—we often forget to laugh. In our Groundhog Day cycles of productivity and performance, laughter can feel like something we "grow out of." Something reserved for late nights with friends or the occasional meme sent in a group chat.

But laughter is the physical embodiment of joy.

When we laugh freely—that full-body, unfiltered expression—we're not just experiencing joy; we're broadcasting it.

It connects us. Realigns us. Grounds us in something more real than perfectionism or pressure.

Some of my most effective, energetic resets have come not through serious introspection, but through sudden, ridiculous, can't-catch-my-breath laughter. These moments reconnect me to that childlike quality of pure joy that lives within all of us.

They don't just lift my mood—they recalibrate my state.
They help me let go.
They help me remember my true self.

## WHY JOY BELONGS IN BUSINESS

You might be wondering: *Why focus on joy in a business book?*

Because joy isn't just a personal state—it's a profoundly professional tool.

When you operate from this high-frequency state:

- Your creativity expands, leading to more innovative solutions
- Your messaging resonates more authentically, attracting aligned clients
- Your decision-making improves as your mind becomes more flexible
- Your resilience strengthens, helping you navigate challenges without burnout
- Your presence becomes naturally magnetic, making sales and connections feel effortless

Joy infuses your brand with an authentic energy that clients and customers can feel. According to researcher Ingrid Fetell Lee, joy attracts others—not through forced positivity, but through real, embodied energy. It makes you more trustworthy. More inspiring. Even more attractive (Lee, 2018).

And when joy expresses itself as laughter in business contexts, it creates psychological safety, especially within teams. Studies show that teams who laugh together perform better, communicate more effectively, and solve problems more creatively. That's because laughter dissolves barriers, creates bonds, and reminds everyone of their shared humanity.

I've experienced this myself—the difference between building from pressure and building from joy. From pushing through a launch with tight shoulders and a clenched jaw to creating from a place of deep inner clarity and spaciousness.

And I can tell you without a doubt: when I'm operating from joy, the results always reflect it.

## YOUR JOY EMERGENCY KIT

When deadlines loom, clients are demanding, and your energy is tanking, try one of these joy-frequency resets:

- Step outside and feel the sun or breeze on your skin for 60 seconds.
- Look at a photo that captures a moment of pure joy from your past.
- Take 3 deep breaths while remembering why you started your business.
- Allow yourself to laugh by watching a short clip that never fails to uplift you.
- Call someone who brings out your playful side.
- Keep a "joy folder" of images, messages, or videos that spark that childlike delight within you.

These aren't escapes from your work—they're strategic vibrational resets that allow you to return to your business at a higher frequency.

Often, the fastest path back to joy is through laughter—that immediate, embodied expression that instantly breaks the pattern of seriousness and reconnects you to your essence.

---

## ◎ TRY THIS

**Your Business Joy Inventory**

Take 5 minutes to reflect:

- What tasks or activities make you lose track of time because you're so engaged?
- Which aspects of your work (past or present) consistently energize rather than drain you?
- What type of client interactions leave you feeling inspired and fulfilled?
- When have you experienced moments where your skills, passion, and purpose came together effortlessly?

These aren't just pleasant memories—they're signposts pointing toward your highest frequency business activities. The areas where your joy and your work intersect are often where your greatest impact and profitability lie.

As you build or evolve your business, intentionally design it to include more of these joy-generating elements. This isn't self-indulgent—it's strategically aligning your business with your highest vibrational state.

**Your Joy Through Laughter List**

In your journal, make a list of 5-10 things that never fail to bring you joy through laughter, even if they're completely silly or unexpected. This might include:

- Favorite comedy clips
- Friends who always make you laugh
- Memories that still bring a smile to your face
- Books or podcasts that lighten your spirit

Then, schedule one into your day. Use it as an intentional joy reset when the energy gets heavy.

**Bonus practice:** Next time something goes wrong—a tech issue, a miscommunication, a small slip-up—pause and ask, "Is there anything about this I'll laugh at later?" If the answer is yes, let yourself laugh now. With just one conscious redirection, frustration can soften—and joy can return almost instantly.

---

## LEADING FROM JOY

Tomorrow morning, try something different.

Before you check emails or jump into strategy, ask yourself: "How can I bring more joy to my leadership today?"

Maybe it's starting team meetings with a genuine moment of connection.
Maybe it's celebrating small wins that usually go unnoticed.
Maybe it's approaching that difficult conversation with openness rather than dread.

This shift—from joy as something you chase to joy as something you embody—redefines not just how you feel, but how you lead.

It's the difference between a business that drains and one that energizes.

Between a team that functions and one that thrives. Between work that pays the bills and work that feeds your soul.

Remember: joy isn't just an emotion. It's a revolutionary business choice.

## CLOSING REFLECTION

You don't have to wait until everything is perfect to feel joy.

In fact, joy might be the very thing that moves everything into harmony.

It invites you back into the moment.

It brings spaciousness to your mind, softness to your body, and connection to your heart.

And here's the most beautiful part—joy builds resilience.

As psychologist Barbara Fredrickson explains, even small moments of joy can initiate upward spirals that enhance our resilience, broaden our perspectives, and reduce stress reactivity (Fredrickson, 2001). These spirals influence how we think, relate, lead, and recover. They help us become more emotionally resilient, more open to possibility, and less reactive to stress.

So, start small.
Start softly.
Start now.
Notice the light.
Welcome the warmth.

Let yourself experience joy in all its expressions—from quiet contentment to full-bodied laughter that bubbles up from your soul.

Because you were never meant to just function.

You were meant to feel alive.

As you begin reconnecting with joy as your natural state, you'll notice how it amplifies your intuition—exactly what we'll explore in the next chapter.

# CHAPTER 5
# THE POWER OF SURRENDER: WHEN LETTING GO BECOMES A BUSINESS STRATEGY

SOME CHANGES HAPPEN LIKE LIGHTNING—THEY strike, and everything changes. Others happen like fog lifting—slow, gentle, but just as profound.

This insight was a fog-lifter for me.

Because for a long time, I didn't realize that much of what I was doing, even in the name of alignment, was still rooted in force. In trying to make things happen. Control outcomes. Push forward no matter the cost.

In his groundbreaking book *Power vs. Force*, Hawkins explains this distinction through vibrational frequencies.

Force is coercive. It's rooted in fear, urgency, pressure, and control. It comes from the outside and needs continual effort to sustain. It's like holding your breath and hoping you can outlast the discomfort.

Power is internal. Clear. Clean. Expansive. It rises from within—rooted in truth, inner coherence, and deep self-trust. It's quiet and grounded. Power doesn't push or shout; it pulls and magnetizes. It leads without needing to dominate, effective through its presence rather than its force.

> "Power appeals to what uplifts, dignifies, and ennobles. Force must always be justified, whereas power requires no justification."
>
> DR DAVID R. HAWKINS

When we operate from power, there's a calm certainty beneath our actions, trust in timing, a connection to truth, and energetic integrity that people can feel—even if they can't name it.

And in business? This distinction is everything. It influences how we launch. How we lead. How we sell. How we serve.

## HOW WE EXPERIENCE THIS DISTINCTION

When you understand vibrational frequency, this difference between power and force becomes undeniable.

When you're operating from force, you might notice:

- Tightness in your chest or jaw
- Overthinking and spiralling
- Hustling with no clear endpoint
- Saying yes when your body is screaming no
- Needing others' responses to feel safe or validated

It's the frequency of survival—of "do more to feel enough."

When you're operating from power, you might feel:

- Calm, even in challenge
- Connected to your intuition
- Decisive without needing to convince others

- Energized rather than depleted by your work
- Detached from outcomes but deeply committed to the process

Power doesn't demand. It radiates. It doesn't prove. It embodies.

And once you become attuned to this energetic difference, it changes everything. You start to feel it in how you launch, how you lead, how you sell, and how you serve—not by force, but by the magnetic pull of aligned inner power. one that changes not just your results, but the way you experience the journey.

## FINDING POWER THROUGH SURRENDER

Here are two questions that changed everything for me:

*How do I move from force to power?*
*What's the bridge between these two states?*

The answer, I discovered, is **surrender**.

Not surrender as in giving up. But surrender, as in letting go of resistance.

I was sitting on the beach one day, watching the waves roll in, trying to calm myself—trying to settle something in my chest that felt impossibly tight. I'd come here hoping that nature would help me exhale because I couldn't seem to find a way through what I was feeling.

There was a situation in my life that I couldn't fix.

And believe me, I'd tried.

I'd strategized. Analysed. Overthought. I'd tried to control the outcome with everything I had—mind, logic, grit. It was the masculine energy I'd learned to master: force it, fix it, push it through.

That's what I knew.

That was how I'd always created results—through action, intensity, and doing.

But this time, it wasn't working.

And I could feel it in my body—the exhaustion, the anxiety, the frustration of trying to force something into place when nothing was responding.

I'd brought Michael Singer's *The Surrender Experiment* with me—a book I was already halfway through. Sitting on the sand, I turned the page to the next chapter.

Its title?

*Acceptance. Acceptance. And More Acceptance.*

It stopped me.

It felt like the universe had reached out and handed me exactly what I needed to hear, at the exact moment I needed to hear it.

The chapter describes a moment when Singer let go of trying to fight what was happening and instead allowed it—not because he agreed with it, not because it felt easy, but because he understood that resistance was only tightening the knot.

Something in me shifted.

Physically. Energetically. Emotionally.

I felt the grip of control begin to loosen.

The pressure to fix, solve, push—it melted, just a little.

That was the day I stopped trying to force my way through.

As I let go of control, all of those feelings of resistance, all those feelings of angst, all the heaviness that was depleting my energy simply dissolved. The situation—whilst it still wasn't what I wanted—hadn't changed at all, but my response to it completely changed. I felt liberated, no longer burdened by circumstances I couldn't change.

That was the beginning of my journey with surrender. And it changed everything.

I realized that surrender was the pathway that takes us from force into true power.

## WHAT SURRENDER REALLY IS

Surrender is often misunderstood—especially by high-achieving women who've been conditioned to associate power with pushing, control with competence, and softness with weakness.

So let's clear something up right now:

Surrender is not giving up.
It's not failure.
It's not passivity, apathy, or inaction.

Surrender is not about abandoning your vision.

It's about releasing the resistance to how that vision unfolds.
It's not about doing nothing.
It's about doing what's needed from a place of grounded state, not anxiety.

When we're trapped in the masculine overdrive of "make it happen," surrender can feel like letting go of control—and it is.

But that's not weakness. That's wisdom.

**And this isn't just spiritual philosophy—it's backed by science.**

When we're in resistance, our bodies produce stress hormones like cortisol that keep us in fight-or-flight. This hijacks our prefrontal cortex—the part of our brain responsible for creative problem-solving and higher reasoning. Research from the HeartMath Institute shows that the state of acceptance actually creates heart-brain coherence, allowing us to access more of our intelligence and intuition.

In other words, surrender doesn't diminish your power—it amplifies it by allowing you to operate from your full cognitive and creative capacity instead of your stress response.

Surrender is choosing to trust energy over force.

It's a transition from efforting to allowing.
From tension to truth.
From force to flow—not by giving up, but by getting out of your own way.

## FORCE VS. POWER IN BUSINESS MOMENTS

Understanding these concepts reshapes how we approach everything in business. Here are some practical distinctions that illustrate the difference between force and power:

**Acceptance vs. Rejection**

When something unexpected happens—a supplier drops out, a launch underperforms, a team member quits—how you respond determines the energy you're operating from.

*Acceptance* is an act of power. It doesn't mean you're happy about what happened—it means you're willing to meet the moment as it is. It's grounded. Flexible. Resilient.

*Rejection*, on the other hand, is rooted in force. It's the inner "this shouldn't be happening" dialogue that leads to stress, contraction, and reactive decision-making. It's fighting what already is—and that fight costs you energy.

**Determination vs. Stubbornness**

***Determination*** is an expression of power. It means staying committed to your vision while remaining open to how it unfolds. It's flexible, adaptive, and responsive—anchored in purpose, not ego.

***Stubbornness***, however, is a form of force. It refuses to change direction. It pushes the same strategy even when the signs are clear that something isn't working. It clings to "the plan" instead of asking, *"What's the most aligned path forward now?"*

I've had seasons when things in my business didn't go according to plan. Massive things went wrong—decisions I had to make and outcomes I couldn't reverse.

And my instinct was to fix it. Fast.

I pushed.
I gripped.
I strategized, re-strategized, worked longer hours, and obsessed over the details.

All in an effort to get things back on track.

But the more I tried to force a solution, the more I disconnected from myself.

I lost sleep. I couldn't think clearly.

The stress wasn't just mental—it was energetic. And I was living in a state of fear, anxiety, and constant pressure.

That's when I began to understand something:

What I thought was helping—the fixing, the pushing, the gripping—was actually pulling me further away from the clarity I needed.

It was lowering my vibration. It was cutting me off from the very thing that had built my business: **alignment**.

---

## ◎ TRY THIS: FROM FORCE TO POWER THROUGH SURRENDER

The key to moving from force to power lies in knowing when you're operating from each state and practicing surrender as the bridge between them.

**1. The Power Decision Filter**

Before making your next business decision, try this simple filter:

*Am I choosing this from clarity or reaction?*
*Does this decision feel expansive or contractive?*
*Would I make this same choice if no one ever knew about it?*
*Is this aligned with my highest values or with my fears?*

Whether it's a difficult decision, a moment of being overwhelmed, or a situation I'm gripping too tightly, I now ask myself:

*Am I coming from power... or from force?*

If I recognize I'm operating from force, it gives me the chance to shift through surrender. To pause. To regulate. To reconnect to my own energetic integrity.

And what I've found—again and again—is that when I choose differently, the resistance often softens. Sometimes, the "thing" that was stuck begins to move. Sometimes a solution appears that I hadn't seen before.

**2. The Surrender Prompt**

Think of an area in your life or business where you've been gripping tightly. Trying to control, fix, force, or figure it all out.

Now, ask yourself:

*What am I afraid will happen if I stop pushing?*
*What might open up if I released my attachment to the outcome?*
*If I trusted that this is happening for me, not to me... what might I do differently?*

Let the answers rise without judgment. Then, write a short surrender statement. One sentence. Something like:

*"I surrender my need to control this launch. I trust that the right people will find it."* or
*"I surrender my fear around this conversation. I trust that truth will guide me."*

Come back to it anytime you feel the grip tightening.

### 3. Power Pulse Check

Over the next week, take a moment at the end of each day and ask yourself:

*Where did I act from power today?*
*Where did I operate from force?*
*What did each one feel like in my body?*

Write your answers down. No judgment—just awareness.

This is how power becomes your baseline—not through more effort but through energetic awareness.

## WHAT SURRENDER LOOKS LIKE IN BUSINESS

Understanding surrender is one thing, but what does it actually look like in daily business operations? Here are some practical examples:

Surrender looks like:

- Saying, "*I don't have to have all the answers right now.*"
- Taking aligned action—and releasing your attachment to how it has to work.
- Letting go of the timeline when it's causing you stress.
- Trusting that the right path will unfold—even if it's different than the one you planned.
- Choosing to believe that a setback isn't punishment—it's redirection.

In practical business terms, this might mean:

- Launching your offer even when it's not "perfect"
- Delegating tasks without micromanaging how they're completed
- Making a decision with the information you have, rather than waiting for absolute certainty
- Adapting your business model when the market changes instead of forcing your original plan

This isn't about inaction. It's about inspired action from a place of trust rather than fear. It's moving from the contracted energy of force into the expansive energy of power.

## CLOSING REFLECTION

You don't need to be louder, push harder, or prove more to be magnetic.

Your true power lives in your energy—not your effort.

It lives in how grounded you are in your truth. In your ability to act with clarity, even when things feel uncertain. In your willingness to trust the process without gripping to the outcome.

Force will always try to convince you that you're not doing enough. That you have to push, rush, prove, or perform.

Power whispers something very different:

You already know.
You're already aligned.
You just need to act from that place.

Surrender is not something we master. It's something we practice—again and again—especially in the moments that stretch us. Because the reality is, life won't always go to plan. Business won't always follow the script. There will be detours. Delays. Disappointments.

But there will also be moments of profound redirection.

Miracles we never could have orchestrated.

Paths that reveal themselves only after we let go of trying to control every step.

Surrender is not a collapse. It's an expansion.

It's a softening into trust, into a deeper intelligence that's already guiding you, even if you can't see it yet.

And the more you choose power over force—in your communication, your leadership, your pricing, your launches, your boundaries—the more your energy will speak for you.

You won't have to chase what's meant for you. You'll attract it. Because you'll be embodying the frequency that creates lasting, soul-aligned success.

## CHAPTER 6
# ENERGY AUDIT: WHAT'S DRAINING YOU, WHAT'S FUELING YOU, AND WHAT NEEDS TO CHANGE

I REMEMBER SITTING at my desk one afternoon, surrounded by business plans, marketing strategies, and to-do lists that stretched into infinity.

My shoulders were tight. My breathing shallow. A faint headache was beginning to pulse at my temples.

My body was sending signals, but I was too focused on my work to listen.

And then, something in me broke the pattern.

Instead of pushing through as I always had, I paused and actually paid attention to what my body was telling me.

That moment marked a profound transition—from ignoring my body's wisdom to honoring it as my most reliable guide. I needed to stop looking at what I was doing and start noticing where my energy was flowing.

Now, as you reach this point in your journey, you've built a solid foundation of energetic understanding.

You've explored your vibrational state.

You've begun to understand the power of joy, the release of laughter, and the difference between force and true inner power.

You've even tasted what surrender might feel like—that subtle shift from control to trust.

And now, we arrive at a natural next step: Looking at where your energy is actually going.

This is the perfect moment to pause and take stock.

To learn the language your body speaks.

To notice those subtle cues before they become alarms—the tightness in your shoulders, the scattered thoughts, the restlessness or fatigue that signal it's time to step away, ground yourself, breathe deeply, or simply rest.

Think of this energy audit as your personalized roadmap, illuminating which aspects of the coming chapters might be most relevant to your unique journey.

This audit will bring awareness to patterns and energy leaks that we'll address directly in the chapters ahead.

Because awareness without action is just a concept.

But awareness paired with clarity and responsibility?

That's power.

This chapter is about getting honest—not in a self-critical way, but in a loving, energetic inventory that invites you to clean up what no longer serves you and realign with what lifts you higher.

## WHAT IS AN ENERGY AUDIT?

Think of it as a vibrational stocktake.

Just as a business reviews its profit and loss or a building undergoes a structural inspection, an energy audit is a check-in with your internal world.

Where is your energy going? What's fuelling you—and what's quietly depleting you? Where are you creating from alignment... and where might you be forcing?

This process isn't about fixing. It's about seeing.

Because once you start noticing what drains you and what energizes you—what expands you and what contracts you—you can begin to make choices that realign your life from the inside out.

You may be ready for an energy audit if...

- You feel like you're constantly "on" but still not making progress
- You struggle to rest, even when you're exhausted
- You're easily triggered or reactive to things that used to feel manageable
- You're doing all the "right" things, but they don't feel aligned
- You've reached the edge of your capacity and don't know what to cut or change

In other words, you're leaking energy.

And you don't need a better productivity system. You need clarity—and the courage to realign.

## CATEGORIES TO REFLECT ON

Use the following categories as prompts. You don't need to audit every area every week, but even one intentional change can create meaningful space.

**Mental Energy**

- What thoughts occupy most of your mind space lately?
- Are they energising or depleting?
- Are you obsessing over something you can't control?
- Are you spending energy battling impostor syndrome or questioning your capabilities when you could be channeling that energy into creation?

**Emotional Energy**

- What emotions feel most dominant right now?
- Where might you be holding unresolved anger, guilt, or fear?
- Are you avoiding emotions by numbing or staying busy?

**Relational Energy**

- Who do you feel nourished by?
- Who consistently drains or confuses you?
- Where are you overgiving or not honoring your boundaries?
- Where might you benefit from seeking mentorship or guidance from someone who's navigated similar challenges?

**Business & Work**

- Which tasks feel aligned and expansive?
- Which feel heavy, but you're still doing them out of obligation or fear?
- Are you building something that still feels like you?

As women entrepreneurs, we often face unique energy drains that can silently deplete our reserves:

- The pressure of wearing multiple hats (CEO, marketer, fulfillment specialist, customer service) without adequate support systems
- The "mental toggle" between business strategic thinking and responsive caregiving roles that many women navigate daily
- The subtle energy drain of code-switching in predominantly male business environments or investor meetings
- The invisible labor of managing not just your business's emotions but often your team's emotional landscape, too
- The weight of perfectionism can be particularly pronounced for women who feel they need flawless execution to be taken seriously

Identifying these specific drains isn't about victimhood—it's about precision. When you can name exactly where your energy is leaking, you can address it with targeted solutions rather than generic "self-care" that doesn't actually solve the root cause.

**Environment & Routine**

- What spaces do you spend the most time in?
- Do they feel inspiring, peaceful, or chaotic?

- What's on your calendar that feels "off" when you tune into it?

## FROM AWARENESS TO ALIGNMENT

This isn't about judging yourself. It's about taking back your energy—lovingly, consciously, and allowing yourself to realign.

You might notice areas where you're still operating from force—doing what you think you "should," gripping to outcomes, or resisting what already is.

This is your opportunity to gently course correct.

Sometimes, the most liberating act is deleting the thing that no longer serves, or finally saying the no you've been sitting on.

And remember: you don't have to fix it all at once. Energetic integrity is built moment by moment in the tiny choices that either drain you... or bring you home to yourself.

---

## ◎ TRY THIS: YOUR ENERGY AUDIT

At the end of this week, block out 30 minutes. Grab a notebook and reflect:

*What gave me energy this week?*
*What drained me?*
*What felt forced?*
*What felt like power—grounded, clear, aligned?*
*What's one thing I can remove, shift, or reclaim next week?*

**Optional**: Use two highlighters—one for "energising" and one for "depleting"—and go through your calendar, inbox, or to-do list. Which color shows up more?

**Your Energy Audit Visualization**

Using *The Energy Audit Wheel* (Figure 6.1), on a scale of 1-10 (with 10 being optimal energy flow), rate yourself in each area:

- **Mental Energy:** How clear, focused, and aligned are your thoughts?
- **Emotional Energy:** How well are you processing feelings rather than suppressing them?
- **Relational Energy:** How nourishing and reciprocal are your key relationships?
- **Business Energy:** How aligned are your daily activities with your vision and values?
- **Environmental Energy:** How supportive are your spaces and routines of your highest self?

Color each segment with your score (1-10) and then you will see a visual representation of your unique energy signature. Where are the dips? The peaks? This visual snapshot often reveals patterns that written reflection alone might miss.

You don't need perfect 10s across the board, but awareness of your current energy distribution empowers you to make intentional adjustments where needed.

You're not just managing time anymore. You're managing energy. And that changes everything.

As you complete your energy audit, you may discover patterns with deeper roots—in your childhood experiences (Chapter 9), hidden addictions (Chapter 10), or language patterns (Chapter 11). The awareness you've gained here will serve as your compass as we explore these areas further.

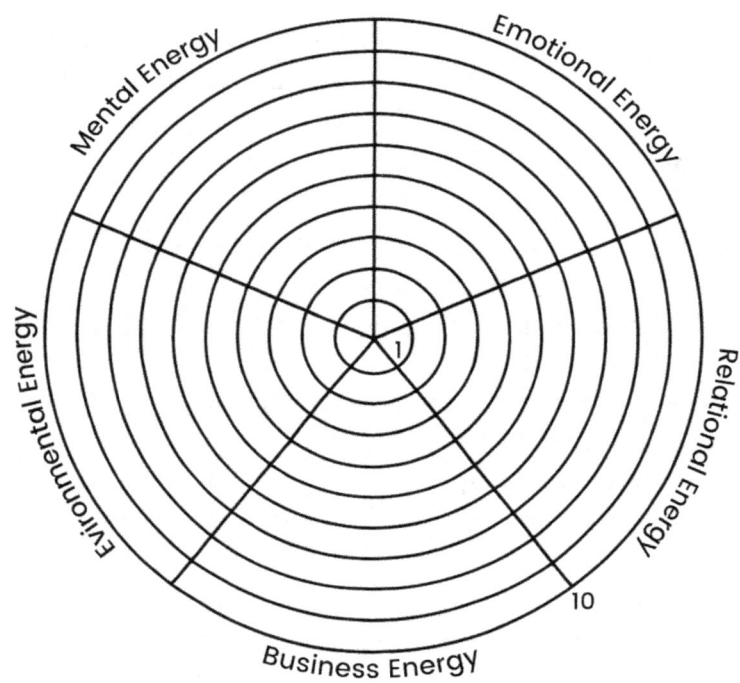

FIGURE 6.1: Energy Audit Wheel

## CLOSING REFLECTION: YOUR ENERGY IS YOUR CURRENCY

This isn't about judging yourself. It's about taking back your energy —lovingly, consciously, and with permission to change.

You might notice areas where you're still operating from force— doing what you think you "should," gripping to outcomes, or resisting what already is.

This is your opportunity to gently course correct.

Sometimes, the most liberating action is deleting the thing that no longer serves, or finally saying the no you've been sitting on.

And remember: transformation isn't instant—it's a series of small, intentional steps. Energetic integrity is built moment by moment—in the tiny choices that either drain you… or bring you home to yourself.

As we move forward, we'll discover how many of these energy patterns are connected to your earliest experiences. In our next chapter, we'll explore healing your inner child—that part of you that still carries old wounds and protective patterns that impact your energy today.

The journey continues—and with each step, you're reclaiming more of your wholeness.

# CHAPTER 7
# INNER CHILD HEALING FOR ALIGNED BUSINESS GROWTH

I WAS WALKING from my office to the kitchen, my mind caught in a loop over a serious business issue I'd been wrestling with for weeks. As I reached the doorway, something in me paused. I became aware of a familiar low-vibrational feeling sitting heavy in my chest.

It wasn't just stress.

When I brought my attention to it, I realized it was resistance.

That sense of pushing against something… instead of flowing with it.

And I recognized it.

In that split-second moment of stillness, I saw what was really going on—I was trying to force an outcome, pushing to "fix" things. My energy was unsettled. And beneath it all, my inner child didn't feel safe.

That's when I realized this feeling was not about the business problem. This resistance, this need to control the outcome, was coming from Little Fe. The part of me that feared failure. The child who learned that not being in control meant danger.

Instead of berating myself for "being blocked," I chose something different.

I softened.

I turned inward and had a quiet, compassionate moment with myself.

"It's okay," I said silently to Little Fe. "I understand why you feel this way. But it's safe now. Let go and trust. I've got this. A solution will come."

It wasn't performative. It wasn't some empty affirmation.

It was real.

And in that moment of honesty and witnessing, the resistance dissolved.

Fifteen minutes later, I returned to my office—clearer, calmer, centred—and opened my inbox.

And there it was. An email waiting for me... with the exact solution I'd been trying so hard to force. You could call it a coincidence. Perhaps. But I know what it really was.

**Alignment. Coherence. A frequency shift. Synchronicity.**

When my inner child felt seen, she let go. And when she let go, everything else began to flow.

This wasn't just mindset. It was energy. It was integration.

It was the part of me that learned to survive by overachieving, finally realising...

She didn't have to do that anymore.

## THE CONNECTION BETWEEN YOUR ENERGY AUDIT AND YOUR INNER CHILD

If the Energy Audit in the last chapter revealed emotional drains that felt deeper than your to-do list, you're likely encountering something fundamental.

The energetic imprint of your earliest years.

Remember in Chapter 2 when we discussed how some of our low vibrational states aren't just about present-moment challenges? How they stem from deeper programs stored from childhood?

This is where those patterns become visible.

And transformable.

What we often label as "self-sabotage," "impostor syndrome," "overwhelm," or "procrastination" is frequently the voice of our inner child.

She's still operating from outdated protection strategies.

Strategies that once kept us safe in a world that felt uncertain or conditional.

## WHO IS THE INNER CHILD?

Your inner child is the energetic imprint of your earliest years—especially the first seven—when your subconscious was wide open and your world was shaped by every glance, tone, absence, and praise.

She internalized the rules of your early world:

- What made you "good"
- What made you "bad"
- What kept you safe
- And what made you lovable

These impressions formed emotional programs that run like subconscious code long into adulthood.

Especially in moments of stress, fear, or exposure.

## HOW SHE SHOWED UP FOR ME

There was a moment I shared in my book *A Scientific Approach to Rewiring Self-Love*—a pattern that frustrated me for years.

During business meetings where I received constructive criticism, tears would spring to my eyes automatically.

As an adult businesswoman, these tears felt inappropriate and overwhelming.

I would get annoyed with myself, thinking, *"Why am I crying? There's no need for this!"*

What I didn't understand then was that by being frustrated with these tears and trying to suppress them, I was being unkind to my inner child.

She had very real reasons to cry in similar situations during childhood. For that little girl, not meeting expectations could have serious consequences.

Her tears weren't an overreaction but a natural response to an environment where being "good" was tied to her safety and survival.

This pattern showed up in other ways, too:

- During challenging business negotiations, where speaking up for my worth would trigger old fears of rejection
- In relationships, where setting boundaries felt frightening because doing so hadn't felt safe in childhood
- When facing uncertainty, particularly around financial

decisions, which brought up childhood anxieties about security
- In moments of conflict, when the urge to people-please and make myself smaller would emerge

Each of these moments wasn't a sign of weakness. It was my inner child's protective patterns being activated.

## THE MANY FACES OF INNER CHILD WOUNDING

Our inner child's beliefs and protective strategies don't just manifest in one way. In business and life, they show up across multiple dimensions:

**Boundary issues**: The inability to say no, chronic overcommitment, and putting others' needs before your own often stem from a child who learned that their worth was tied to pleasing others.

**Self-worth challenges**: Undercharging for your services, apologizing unnecessarily, or feeling guilty for success can all be traced to early programming about what you deserve.

**Self-sabotage patterns**: Procrastination, perfectionism, and avoiding visibility are frequently protective mechanisms your inner child developed to stay "safe."

**Trust and control issues**: Difficulty delegating, micromanaging, or refusing to ask for help often comes from a child who learned they could only rely on themselves.

**And yes, impostor syndrome**: That persistent feeling you don't belong or aren't qualified, despite evidence to the contrary.

None of these patterns exist in isolation. They're interconnected aspects of how your inner child learned to navigate the world.

For years, I couldn't understand why, despite building a successful business and receiving consistent external validation, I still felt like an impostor waiting to be discovered.

The disconnect between my achievements and my internal experience was baffling.

And exhausting.

## THE INNER CHILD AND IMPOSTOR SYNDROME

When we look at impostor syndrome through the lens of inner child work, we come to an important realization: it's not that we don't believe in our adult capabilities. It's that our inner child doesn't believe she's allowed to be powerful, visible, or successful.

She's operating from an outdated playbook where staying small meant staying safe.

My research for this book, along with studies such as the 2020 KPMG Women's Leadership Summit Report, revealed that 75% of high-performing women in business have experienced impostor syndrome at some point in their careers. What's more, 85% of these women believe impostor syndrome is commonly experienced by women in business.

The research also found that 81% of these women believe they put more pressure on themselves not to fail than men do, and 74% believe their male counterparts don't experience the same levels of self-doubt.

In this same study, nearly half (47%) of high-performing women reported that their feelings of self-doubt result from never expecting to reach the level of success they have achieved. This disconnect between childhood expectations and adult reality is exactly where our inner child gets confused.

What I eventually realized was that this wasn't about my current capabilities or achievements at all.

It was about the little girl inside me who'd learned that safety came from being perfect. From achieving. From making sure everyone else was happy with her.

When we feel like impostors in our businesses, struggle with boundaries, and sabotage our success just as it's within reach, we're often experiencing our inner child's discomfort with standing in her power.

She's running old programs that associate visibility with danger. Success with unwanted attention. Achievement with the pressure to keep performing perfectly.

No amount of external validation can fix these patterns because they live in our nervous system, in our emotional body, in the beliefs we formed before we even had words.

## HOW THIS MAY BE SHOWING UP FOR YOU

Inner child wounding doesn't always look like trauma.

For successful entrepreneurs, it often manifests as:

- Perfectionism that delays launches and exhausts you
- Difficulty delegating because "no one will do it right"
- Undercharging despite delivering exceptional value
- Overworking to prove your worthiness
- Hesitancy to celebrate wins because "it's never enough"
- A persistent feeling of fraudulence when stepping into visibility
- Struggling to set and maintain boundaries
- Putting others' needs before your own – even when it harms your business

- Avoiding difficult conversations that could move your business forward
- Fear of outshining others or being "too much"

You might recognize her voice in thoughts like:

- *"Who am I to be doing this?"*
- *"If I slow down, everything will fall apart."*
- *"They'll leave if I'm not useful."*
- *"It's not safe to take up space."*
- *"I can't say no – they'll be disappointed."*
- *"I should be able to handle everything myself."*

These aren't character flaws or signs you're not cut out for success. They're protective adaptations from a time when these beliefs may have served you.

And they can be healed—gently, consciously, energetically.

## WHAT THE SCIENCE SAYS

Both Dispenza and Lipton affirm what I came to understand through my own healing journey. Dispenza teaches that repetitive thoughts and emotions from the past train the body to stay in a memorized emotional state.

Your inner child may no longer be in danger, but your body hasn't received the memo yet.

This explains why self-limiting patterns can persist despite external success.

Regardless of your current achievements or capabilities, your nervous system still operates from old emotional patterning.

Lipton adds that these beliefs don't just shape our minds; they influence our biology. His work in epigenetics shows that subconscious programs from childhood impact gene expression, behavior, and health.

And the empowering truth? We can rewrite them.

Through meditation and conscious awareness practices, we can bypass the analytical mind, access new emotional states, and rewire the neural pathways tied to those old survival patterns.

This is the bridge between self-awareness and science—and it's where real change begins..

## FOUR ELEMENTS OF INNER CHILD HEALING FOR ENTREPRENEURS

**1. Acknowledgment**: Recognize that your inner child is still influencing how you show up in your business—not to shame her, but to free her.

***My experience***: I began noticing when "Little Fe" was driving my decisions. Was I avoiding that sales call because it wasn't strategic or because my inner child feared rejection? This awareness alone created space for choice.

**2. Communication**: Speak to her with curiosity. Journal, meditate, or simply ask: *"What are you afraid of right now?"* Let her speak.

***My experience***: Before important negotiations, I would take a moment to check in: *"What does Little Fe need to feel safe right now?"* Often, she just needed reassurance that my worth wasn't tied to the outcome.

**3. Compassion and Support**: Reassure her that she no longer needs to protect you through overworking, hiding, or shrinking. You've got her now.

***My experience:*** When tears would arise during feedback sessions, instead of pushing them away, I'd inwardly acknowledge: *"I see you're scared. That's okay. Adult Fiona has this handled."*

**4. Reparenting**: Start making decisions as the adult she needed: One who sets boundaries. One who rests. One who believes she is enough.

***My experience:*** I began consciously choosing actions that contradicted my inner child's fears—resting when she urged me to keep pushing, speaking up when she wanted to stay small, and celebrating wins when she whispered I hadn't done enough.

## FROM LIMITATION TO LIBERATION

As I practiced these elements, something remarkable happened.

The persistent patterns of self-limitation began to dissolve. Not because I achieved more or pushed harder, but because I stopped abandoning the part of me that felt unsafe in success.

By healing my relationship with my inner child:

- I could receive praise without deflecting it
- I set prices that reflected my true value
- I made decisions from present capability rather than past fears
- I stepped into visibility without the crushing anxiety that once accompanied it
- I established boundaries without guilt or over-explanation
- I recognized my worth wasn't tied to constant productivity
- I allowed myself to celebrate success without waiting for the other shoe to drop

This shift wasn't just psychological—it was energetic.

The energy once consumed by maintaining those protective patterns became available for creation, innovation, and authentic leadership.

This is where inner child healing becomes essential. We learn to become that supportive voice for ourselves—the one who sees our value inherently, not just for what we achieve.

---

## ⊚ TRY THIS: A GENTLE CHECK-IN FOR TRIGGERING MOMENTS

The next time you feel that familiar contraction—whether it's impostor syndrome before a presentation, boundary challenges with a client, or self-sabotage as you approach a milestone—try this:

Take a quiet moment. Place your hand on your heart. Breathe.

Ask yourself:

*"What does the little girl in me need to hear right now?"*

Then, speak back to her with love:

*"You're safe now."*
*"You don't have to earn it anymore."*
*"You matter, just as you are."*
*"Your needs are important too."*
*"It's okay to take up space."*

Even a few honest words can raise your frequency and release the energy being consumed by these old patterns.

---

## ! A NOTE ON SUPPORT & SCOPE

Inner child healing is sacred work, but it can also bring up deep emotions or memories that extend far beyond the scope of any book.

What I've shared are entry points and gentle practices that have helped me personally, but I want to acknowledge that true inner child healing—especially for those with significant trauma—often requires dedicated, professional support over time.

If what arises feels overwhelming as you explore these concepts, please seek support from a trauma-informed coach, therapist, or space-holder. There is no shame in needing help. This is leadership.

The journey of reconnecting with and healing your inner child is unique for everyone. For some, it might be a relatively straightforward process of reconnection. For others, it may be an intensive, multi-year journey requiring specialized support.

This chapter offers tools to begin this conversation with yourself, but it doesn't replace the depth of work that might be needed. Honor your unique path and timeline.

*Remember:* Healing doesn't happen on a schedule or through a checklist. It unfolds in its own time, with the right support, and with deep self-compassion.

## CLOSING REFLECTION: FROM INNER CHILD TO EMPOWERED LEADER

Your inner child doesn't need to be "fixed." She is craving to be witnessed.

When you meet her with love instead of control, she softens. And when she softens, your adult self can finally lead—with confidence, compassion, and coherence.

This is how you become the woman you were always meant to be. Not by pushing her away. But by welcoming her home.

This integration alchemises limitation into liberation, not by denying your vulnerability but by embracing all parts of yourself as you step into your full power as a leader, creator, and force for change.

In the chapters ahead, we'll explore how these childhood patterns connect to hidden addictions that keep us playing small, the language patterns that reinforce our limitations, and how to develop your intuitive intelligence beyond these old constraints.

# CHAPTER 8
# UNVEILING HIDDEN ADDICTIONS THAT HOLD YOU—AND YOUR BUSINESS—BACK

FLASHBACK TO 2022. I had been experiencing chronic migraines for 36 years.

Not just the occasional headache...

We're talking four to five migraines every month, each one lasting two to four days at a time. The kind of pain that completely derails your plans, clouds your mind, and keeps you in a constant loop of recovery.

And I had tried everything.

Naturopathy. Neurology. Pharmaceuticals. Physiotherapy. Chiropractic. Diet changes. Supplements. Movement. And more. Some things offered temporary relief. Most didn't. Nothing brought real, lasting change.

I'd made peace with the idea that this was just something I'd live with—a condition I'd always have to manage.

And then, in 2022, I found myself sitting in a room full of entrepreneurs at Dr. Espen's *Conscious Enterprise Retreat*.

We were talking about business, and more specifically, about what blocks us from rising. How unconscious addictions—even subtle ones—can hold entrepreneurs back from their true potential.

At first, I didn't think it applied to me.

I don't drink excessively. I've never had a substance issue. I'm not addicted to sugar or scrolling. I thought, *"I'm in the clear."*

But then Espen looked me straight in the eyes and said something I'll never forget:

*"Sometimes, the most powerful addiction isn't to a substance. It's to a **story you tell yourself.**"*

And it landed in my body like lightning.

I knew, in that instant, what mine was.

***"I am a migraine sufferer."***

It had become more than a symptom. It had become a belief, an identity, a loop I was stuck in—not just physically but energetically.

## ADDICTION AS IDENTITY

When we repeat something often enough, it becomes how we see ourselves.

*"I am anxious."*
*"I am burnt out."*
*"I am a procrastinator."*
*"I am always tired."*
*"I am a migraine sufferer."*

Not *"I feel..."*
Not *"I'm experiencing..."*

But *"I **am**..."*

These aren't just phrases. They are energetic commitments.

And as long as we stay committed to them—consciously or not—our energy, biology, and behaviour continue to reinforce them.

That day, sitting at that retreat, I realized I had been carrying the frequency of suffering for most of my life.

Not because I wanted to. But because, as a child growing up in a home where there was violence and unpredictability, suffering was familiar.

I learned to suffer silently, invisibly. To endure the pain at home, then go to school or ballet class as if nothing were wrong. To keep my worlds separate through quiet endurance.

And later, migraines became the perfect physical expression of this pattern—an invisible suffering that no one could see but that consumed my inner world, not like a broken leg or visible wound, but a silent pain that others couldn't witness or validate.

So, it made sense that eventually, that energy had to go somewhere. It found its home in my body. In migraines—the perfect physical manifestation of my silent suffering. Pain that remained invisible to others yet consumed my entire being. A continuation of the pattern I'd learned so well: suffering that no one could see.

So, that day at the retreat, I realized that the pattern no longer belonged to me.

And I chose to release it.

I made a decision: From that moment forward, I would stop saying, *"I am a migraine sufferer."*

And I haven't had a migraine since.

Do I have scientific proof that changing this one statement cured my migraines? Not exactly.

But after 36 years of "suffering"—after trying everything possible to cure myself—the only thing that changed was my relationship with this identity.

The weight of evidence certainly points toward something profound: Our identities create our biology. Our stories become our physical reality.

My later research into epigenetics taught me that our thoughts and beliefs create an environment around our cells that influences which genes get expressed and which remain dormant. By releasing the identity "I am a migraine sufferer" to simply being me, I'd altered the energetic landscape of my entire system. I had switched off the genetic expression for migraines.

That one decision gave me back my health, my presence, and my joy.

And with it—my freedom.

## RETHINKING WHAT ADDICTION REALLY IS

My story about migraines raises a compelling perspective about addiction.

When we hear the word *addiction*, we often think of substances or behaviors that have obvious harmful impacts—alcohol, drugs, gambling, porn, social media. These are the addictions we can easily identify and label.

But what if addiction runs much deeper than that? What if addiction is any repetitive pattern that numbs us from discomfort, distracts us from presence, or keeps us looping in old survival states?

What if addiction is:

- Being chronically busy
- Overthinking
- Seeking validation
- Always fixing others
- Overworking
- Saying "yes" when we mean "no"
- Telling ourselves the same story, over and over again

Most of the time, we're not addicted to the behaviour. We're addicted to what it helps us avoid.

## WHAT ARE YOU PROTECTING?

Addiction is often a trauma response. A way to avoid feeling what was once too overwhelming to process.

It protects. It soothes. It fills space. It helps us feel in control.

And it serves us... until it doesn't.

That's why awareness is the first step. Because you can't change what you won't see.

---

## ◎ TRY THIS: SPOT THE STORY

Take a moment to reflect on the "I am" statements you tell yourself regularly:

*"I am always..."*
*"I am never..."*
*"I am the person who..."*
*"I am bad at..."*
*"I am not capable of..."*

"I am a…"

Write down 3-5 of these statements that feel most familiar.

For each statement, ask yourself:

- Is this objectively true, or is it just a story I've rehearsed?
- When did I first begin telling myself this?
- What emotion or experience is this identity protecting me from?
- If I released this story, how might it redefine the way I lead or build my business?

You don't need to rush to change anything. Simply witnessing these patterns with compassion is the first step toward freedom.

The power lies in recognition, not judgment.

## SHIFTING THE FREQUENCY

Letting go of the migraine story wasn't just a mindset shift. It was a vibrational shift.

My body stopped identifying with pain. My energy no longer aligned with suffering. I began speaking a new reality into being.

I didn't need more medications. I needed to tell myself the truth:

*"This story has served me. But I don't need it anymore."*

Through my work with Dr. Espen, I came to understand this process wasn't merely psychological—it was neurobiological. These identity-based stories become wired into our neural pathways. Each time we repeat "I *am* [limitation]," we strengthen those neural connections, creating a manifestation of our limiting beliefs.

But the reverse is also true: When we consciously interrupt those patterns and create new ones, we begin rewiring our brain for possibility rather than limitation.

What began as a personal breakthrough soon sent ripples through every area of my life. It fundamentally changed how I show up as an entrepreneur. And this is true regardless of what your particular addiction might be - whether it's an identity story like mine, chronic busyness, perfectionism, people-pleasing, or any of the subtler addictions we often don't recognize.

Think about how your addiction impacts your business right now:

- How much creative energy is being diverted to maintaining it?
- How often does it interfere with your decision-making?
- In what ways does it limit your ability to show up fully for your team or clients?
- How might it be holding you back from taking necessary risks?

When we release these patterns—whatever form they take—we free up massive amounts of energy that can now flow into our vision, our teams, and our impact. We remove invisible barriers to our success that no business strategy alone could overcome.

The entrepreneur who releases their addiction to approval becomes capable of making bold, necessary decisions. The founder who lets go of perfectionism suddenly finds the courage to launch before everything is "ready." The leader who stops identifying as 'always overwhelmed' discovers untapped reservoirs of creativity and clarity.

Your business will only rise as high as your energy allows. Free your energy from these addictive patterns, and watch what becomes possible.

## CLOSING REFLECTION

We don't always realize what we're addicted to.

Sometimes, it's not the thing we consume—it's the identity we carry. The role we play. The narrative we've built our sense of self around.

Once it's seen, it no longer holds the same power—you can choose differently.

. And by realigning your energy, you change your vibration, and that, in turn, changes everything.

You don't have to rip the story away. You just have to ask:

*"Is this still true for me?"*
*"Is it time to write a new one?"*

Your body will know. Your energy will respond. And your next chapter will begin—from a place of sovereignty, not suffering.

## CHAPTER 9
# REFRAMING YOUR LANGUAGE: THE WORDS THAT LIMIT YOUR RESULTS

I USED to speak about money as if it were an outsider.

Something separate from me. Something just out of reach. Something I wanted—but didn't fully believe was mine to claim.

I thought I was doing all the right things. Writing down my financial goals. Placing affirmations around my home. Speaking them out loud in the present tense.

But one day, as I walked past one of those affirmations—*"I am financially free"*—I heard a whisper inside my head.

*"Yeah, but you probably won't achieve that."*

It stopped me in my tracks.

I was shocked at how casual the thought was. How subtle. And how familiar.

That voice had been there all along, overriding every affirmation, quietly programming my subconscious with the exact frequency I was working so hard to release.

That was the day I realized I wasn't just speaking my intentions. I was also speaking about my limitations.

## WORDS ARE MORE THAN JUST SOUND

Your language isn't just communication. It's code.

Every word you speak reinforces your beliefs. And your beliefs shape your energetic state.

*"I can't afford that."*
*"No one will pay that much."*
*"It's just so hard."*
*"I'm not ready yet."*
*"People like me don't..."*
*"You have to have money to make money."*
*"I'm not good with finances."*
*"That's too expensive."*
*"I just want to help people—I'm not in it for the money."*

These seemingly innocent phrases aren't just habits of speech—they're energetic programming with measurable impacts on your neurochemistry and electromagnetic field.

They shape your posture.
Your pricing.
Your decisions.

They tell your nervous system how safe you are to receive.

## WHAT THE SCIENCE SAYS

Dispenza's research demonstrates how words create electromagnetic signals that influence our brain's neural architecture. When we repeatedly speak specific phrases, we're not just communicating ideas—we're creating energetic patterns that become encoded in our cells.

These patterns don't stay isolated in the brain. They generate specific frequencies that extend beyond our physical body, creating what quantum physics describes as a "field effect." This field becomes our energetic signature, attracting experiences that match its resonance.

In quantum terms, our words become observers that collapse probability waves into specific realities. The language we use selects which version of reality we experience from infinite possibilities.

What you say, you become. And what you repeatedly say, you embody.

## THE COLLECTIVE LANGUAGE OF BUSINESS

This quantum effect doesn't just impact us individually—it shapes our entire business ecosystem.

The language we use in team meetings creates an energetic container for what's possible. The words in our marketing materials broadcast specific frequencies to potential clients. How we speak about our industry determines what opportunities we can perceive.

I've watched real change unfold when leaders replaced old language patterns—letting go of phrases like:

*"The market is too saturated."*
*"We can't compete with larger companies."*
*"That client is too big for us."*
To language that opens fields of possibility:
*"We bring unique value to this market."*
*"Our size gives us the agility larger companies lack."*
*"We're ready to serve clients at every level."*

These aren't just motivational phrases—they're vibrational agreements that expand or contract the possibilities for your entire organization.

When a team collectively speaks in the frequency of possibility, they begin operating in a completely different reality than competitors who remain trapped in limitation language.

When I mentor entrepreneurs, one of the first things I listen for is their language.

How do they speak about money? About their clients? Their success? Their sense of worth?

Often, they're not aware of the words they're using.

*"I know it's probably too much, but..."*
*"I just hope someone buys it."*
*"I could never charge that."*
*"I don't want to seem greedy."*
*"I'm not great at selling."*

I gently pause them. Not to correct but to empower.

Because once you see the words, you can change them. And when you change them, everything else begins to shift.

## FROM SCARCITY TO SOVEREIGNTY: A PERSONAL REFRAME

Here are a few phrases I used to say (or silently think)—and how I chose to reframe them.

Every time I spoke the new language—even when it felt awkward—I was retraining my frequency. Reprogramming my subconscious. Choosing a new energetic standard.

### TABLE 8.1 REFRAMING LANGUAGE ABOUT MONEY

| Old Language | New Language |
|---|---|
| "I can't afford that." | "That's not aligned for me right now—and that's okay." |
| "It's too expensive." | "It's a premium investment—is it worth it to me?" |
| "I'm not good with money." | "I'm learning how to build a beautiful relationship with money." |
| "Money doesn't grow on trees." | "Money flows to me through value, energy, and alignment." |
| "You have to have money to make money." | "Creative energy and aligned strategy open doors to wealth." |
| "I can't charge that much." | "I'm allowed to be well compensated for the value I offer." |
| "People like me don't get rich." | "I'm creating a new generational story about wealth." |

## TRY THIS: SHIFT THE PHRASE

Take a moment and write down 5 things you've said recently about:

- Money
- Your abilities
- Your business
- Your time
- Your value

Now, pick the one that feels most limiting.

Ask yourself:

*"If this phrase were a code, what result is it generating?"*
*"What belief is it reinforcing?"*
*"What would I rather program instead?"*

Then, rewrite it.

Say it. Speak it. Use it.

At first, it might feel weird. Foreign. Even false.

But keep going. You're not just changing your words—you're changing your reality.

---

## CLOSING REFLECTION

Your language isn't just communication. It's creation.

Each word you speak is casting a spell—literally "spelling" your future into existence.

When you change your speech from limitation to possibility, you're not just changing semantics. You're rewiring neural pathways. You're tuning your electromagnetic frequency. You're altering the very field that attracts your experiences.

This isn't metaphorical—it's quantum.

The entrepreneur who speaks from abundance creates different opportunities than the one who speaks from scarcity. The woman who declares her value attracts different clients than the one who apologizes for her rates.

Your mouth speaks what your mind believes, and your life becomes what your words decree.

So, notice your language patterns. Interrupt them consciously. And choose words that align with the woman you're becoming, not the one you've been programmed to be.

A single moment of awareness can change your business, your relationships, and your inner landscape almost overnight.

Your words are building your world. Make them magnificent.

## CHAPTER 10
# THE MIRROR PRINCIPLE: YOUR BUSINESS REFLECTS WHAT YOU BELIEVE ABOUT YOURSELF

THE FIRST TIME I heard this concept—that what we experience on the outside is often just a mirror of what's happening on the inside—it was confronting. And completely liberating.

But I'll be honest—when I first heard about this principle, I didn't particularly like it.

Looking at my external world, with its challenges and struggles, the idea that all of this somehow reflected my internal state felt almost accusatory. If I was experiencing things I didn't want, was that my fault?

It felt too simple, too convenient an explanation. Too much responsibility to bear.

But when I chose to be real and raw with myself, when I developed a deeper understanding of what this concept truly meant, I discovered it wasn't about blame at all.

It was a superpower that gave me answers.

Because if your external world reflects your internal state... That means you have more power than you think.

## LIFE DOESN'T JUST HAPPEN TO YOU

This wasn't just my personal epiphany. It was a doorway into understanding how consciousness actually creates reality. Science has begun to validate what ancient wisdom traditions have known for centuries: our perception shapes our reality in meaningful and measurable ways.

Our brains process approximately 400 billion bits of information every second, but our conscious mind can only handle about 2,000 bits. This means we're filtering out 99.9999% of available information at any given moment.

What determines this filter? Our beliefs, expectations, and emotional patterns.

Neuroscientists refer to this as the reticular activating system (RAS) —the part of the brain that determines what information reaches your conscious awareness. When your RAS is programmed to look for evidence of "I'm not good enough," you'll spot every piece of feedback that confirms this belief while missing evidence to the contrary.

By now, you've explored your energetic nature. You've started noticing how vibrational states influence your choices and results.

This next piece will connect those dots even more deeply:

Your life is always speaking to you. The question is—***are you listening?***

## THE FREQUENCY ALIGNMENT: WHY DESIRES AND REALITY MUST MATCH

One of the most illuminating concepts I learned through my work with Dr. Espen was a visual metaphor that forever changed how I understand manifestation.

Imagine two energy frequencies represented as lines—one showing where you currently vibrate emotionally and another showing the frequency of what you're trying to create.

When these frequencies aren't aligned, they remain separate paths that never intersect. This explains why we can want something desperately while continuing to create its opposite.

I saw this clearly in my own life. I desired deep, meaningful partnerships, but kept experiencing disconnection. My conscious desires and my subconscious programming were operating at completely different frequencies.

This misalignment wasn't a failure of desire or effort; it was simply energetic physics. You cannot tune into a radio station broadcasting at one frequency while your receiver is set to another.

## WHAT TRIGGERS YOU TEACHES YOU

This frequency concept directly connects to how the mirror principle operates in our daily lives. When something in your external world triggers an emotional response, it's often highlighting a frequency mismatch.

Have you ever been annoyed at someone for being disorganized, only to realize you feel out of control internally?

Ever judged someone for being too loud, only to uncover a part of yourself that doesn't feel safe to be seen?

That's the mirror in action.

In your business:

That client who constantly questions your expertise? She might be reflecting your own hidden impostor syndrome.

The team member who keeps missing deadlines? Perhaps mirroring your own struggle with boundaries.

The price point you can't seem to commit to? Possibly reflecting your internal uncertainty about your value.

The people who frustrate you, the situations that activate you—they're not the problem. They're messengers.

Your reactions are reflections. And your resistance reveals what's ready to be healed.

## NOTHING IS RANDOM—EVERYTHING IS FEEDBACK

Once you understand the mirror principle, you begin to see every interaction as valuable feedback about your internal state.

If a client's conversation rattles me? I pause.
If someone's energy throws me off? I check in.
If I find myself judging or withdrawing? I don't just "push through."

I ask:

*What is this reflecting back to me?*
*Is there an unmet need here?*
*What am I being asked to see more clearly?*

This is emotional maturity. Energetic maturity. And leadership maturity.

## THE QUANTUM PERSPECTIVE

The mirror concept extends beyond psychology into quantum physics. Research suggests that the act of observation affects the behavior of energy and matter at the subatomic level—the famous "observer effect."

Dispenza explains that we attract *not what we want* but **what we are**. Our thoughts and feelings emit frequencies that shape what we experience.

Like attracts like. Chaos attracts chaos. Calm attracts opportunity. Scarcity attracts friction. Abundance attracts flow.

When you raise your baseline vibration—through joy, love, self-trust—your outer world begins to reflect those qualities back to you.

It's not magic. It's magnetism.

## REAL TALK: THE MIRROR ISN'T ALWAYS COMFORTABLE

Understanding this principle can be both empowering and challenging but let me be clear: this chapter isn't about blame. It's about radical self-awareness.

There's a crucial distinction between responsibility and fault. Taking responsibility for how your internal state affects your external reality doesn't mean blaming yourself for every circumstance in your life.

Sometimes, the mirror reflects beauty and alignment. Other times, it reflects avoidance, fear, or patterns that need to shift.

But when can you meet that mirror with compassion instead of defensiveness?

That's where the healing begins.

And the beautiful thing is—when you change what's going on within, the world around you recalibrates to meet you there.

## IN BUSINESS, THE MIRROR IS EVERYWHERE

I used to find it incredibly frustrating when potential clients would try to barter over prices or tell me my offers were "too expensive." No matter how much value I stacked or how many testimonials I shared, there always seemed to be pushback.

Eventually, I stopped looking outward and started looking inward. That's when I realized the pattern wasn't about them—it was about me. I didn't fully value what I brought to the table. I undercharged. I overdelivered. And deep down, I questioned whether what I offered was truly *worth* the investment.

When I began to own my worth, everything changed. I raised my prices to honour the breakthroughs I was facilitating. I stopped defending the value—because I *embodied* it. And just like that, the pushback disappeared.

One of my mentors once told me: *"The world will take you at your own valuation."*

That lesson changed everything. Business became a mirror, reflecting where I still needed to step up, speak up, and stand tall in what I believed about myself.

It was never just about pricing. It was about worth.

---

## ◎ TRY THIS: SPOT THE MIRROR

This week, notice what triggers or irritates you—and pause before reacting.

Instead, ask:

*What emotion is this stirring in me?*
*What belief might be getting activated?*
*Is this situation mirroring something I need to look at within myself?*

And then, with love, thank it.

That trigger? That moment? That discomfort?

It's pointing you toward your next layer of growth.

For your business specifically, pay attention to:

- **Client patterns:** Are you attracting the same challenging clients repeatedly?
- **Financial blocks:** Where do you feel resistance around money?
- **Team dynamics:** What qualities in others trigger you?
- **Visibility comfort:** Does marketing feel easy or challenging?

---

## CLOSING REFLECTION: FROM REFLECTION TO RESPONSIBILITY

This principle forms a critical foundation for everything else we'll explore in this book.

The mirror isn't about blame. It's about access points for growth.

When you understand that your external reality offers constant feedback about your internal state, you're no longer at the mercy of circumstances. You recognize your inherent power to reshape your experience from the inside out.

In the coming chapters, we'll build on this understanding—exploring how to consciously direct your energy, rewire limiting beliefs, and create new patterns that better serve your life and business.

You're not merely responding to life. You're creating it. Choice by choice. Thought by thought. Frequency by frequency.

You are not powerless. You are not behind. You are not broken.

You're just waking up.

To who you are. To what you carry. And to the power you have to transform it all—from the inside out.

# INTEGRATION POINT: WHERE AWARENESS BECOMES POWER

You've come to a pivotal threshold.

In these first nine chapters, you've peeled back layers of awareness around the subtle forces that shape your reality as an entrepreneur.

The unconscious frequencies you've been broadcasting.
The stories you've been living as identity.
The words you've been using as code.
The energetic patterns that have shaped your business results.

This awareness isn't just intellectual—*it's vibrational.*

With each realization, with each moment of recognition, you're already tuning into a new frequency. Perhaps you've noticed subtle changes:

- Moments of catching yourself in old patterns.
- A new pause before speaking limiting words.
- A growing awareness of how your energy affects your outcomes.
- A recognition of what no longer serves your vision.

This is the unseen foundation of deep personal evolution.

Most business strategies focus exclusively on what to do. But you now understand a deeper insight: *who you're **being** determines what you can achieve.*

No amount of strategic action can overcome misaligned energy. No marketing tactic can override an identity addiction. No business plan can outperform your vibrational setpoint.

You've done the inner work that most entrepreneurs skip past in their rush toward external results.

And that changes everything about what comes next.

## THE ENERGETIC TURNING POINT

Before we move forward, take a moment to honor what you've uncovered:

- You've recognized the quantum nature of your entrepreneurial journey—how your thoughts, emotions, and energy create your business reality through resonance and frequency.
- You've identified patterns that have shaped your results—unconscious addictions, limiting beliefs, and defensive mechanisms that once served you but now hold you back.
- You've noticed your language patterns and begun reframing your relationship with money, success, and your own abilities.
- You've started questioning identities you've carried that limit your expansion and creativity.

This awareness is already restructuring your neural pathways, creating the biological foundation for new behaviors and results.

You've expanded. Your awareness is deeper, your lens wider—and the way you see yourself and your business has already begun to evolve.

## THE ALCHEMY OF TRANSFORMATION

But awareness alone, while powerful, is just the beginning.

Real change begins when awareness becomes consistent, aligned action through daily practices that rewire the nervous system and anchor a higher frequency.

Many entrepreneurs make the mistake of trying to force change through willpower alone. They push themselves toward new habits without addressing the energetic foundation beneath them.

The result? Burnout. Resistance. Backsliding into old patterns.

You're taking a different approach—one that honors the quantum nature of change:

First, shift the energy. Then, embody the practices. Finally, watch as your external results naturally align.

This is the pathway of the conscious entrepreneur—the leader who understands that business success is an inside-out process.

## THE PATH OF EMBODIMENT

In the coming chapters, we'll explore the daily practices that will stabilize your new frequency—from morning rituals that set your energetic tone to conscious consumption that nourishes your vibration.

These aren't just productivity hacks or wellness tips.

They're quantum technologies—deliberate ways of engaging with energy, time, and physical reality that reprogram your electromagnetic field and create a new baseline for your life and business.

Each practice builds upon the foundation of awareness you've established, translating insight into embodiment.

The difference between those who truly rise and those who remain stuck isn't knowledge—**it's integration.**

It's the daily commitment to living in energetic alignment with your highest vision.
It's the consistent choice to operate from possibility rather than limitation.
It's the courage to let your actions reflect your awakened understanding.

## CROSSING THE THRESHOLD

As we prepare to cross this threshold together, take a moment to reflect:

- What has been your most significant insight from Part I?
- How has your understanding of yourself as an energetic deepened or evolved?
- What old patterns or identities are you now ready to release?
- What new possibility feels most alive in you now?

These questions aren't just reflective exercises; they're activations. By consciously acknowledging your evolution, you're creating coherence between your awareness and what comes next.

You're preparing yourself to not just learn about aligned practices but to embody them fully.

Trust that the awareness you've cultivated is already working within you, creating an energetic readiness for the practical tools that follow.

Your business is about to experience the change that makes all the difference—from operating as a conventional entrepreneur to embracing your role as an energetic leader.

The foundation is set. Now, let's build upon it.

## MAKE A DIFFERENCE WITH YOUR REVIEW - HELP OTHERS RISE

*"When one woman rises, she creates a path for others to follow."*

Female entrepreneurs who share their stories of transformation create ripples of change in the business world.

Let's amplify these ripples together! Would you help someone just like you—a woman ready to build a business aligned with her soul's purpose but unsure where to begin?

My mission is to make the entrepreneurial journey accessible for women by bridging practical business strategy with energetic intuitive flow. To reach more women with this message, I need your help.

Most entrepreneurs discover resources through reviews. Your honest words could be the beacon that guides another woman to her own business breakthrough. Your review could help...

...one more entrepreneur break free from impostor syndrome
...one more business owner heal from burnout
...one more woman discover her leadership voice
...one more visionary understand her unique value

To make a difference, simply scan the QR code and leave a review.

Your review might be exactly what someone needs to hear to begin their own journey of rising in business and life. Thank you for being part of this ripple of transformation!

With gratitude,

*Fiona xx*

# PART TWO
# THE SHIFT

# CHAPTER 11
# MORNING RITUALS FOR CENTERED, HIGH-FREQUENCY WORKDAYS

THERE WAS a time in my life when mornings were pure chaos.

I'd wake up already behind. My mind would start racing before my feet hit the floor. I'd check my phone, open emails, scroll socials, and plunge straight into everyone else's energy—long before I'd connected with my own.

By 9 a.m., I hadn't even paused to ask myself how I was feeling. I was running a business, parenting, responding, reacting—but never truly anchoring.

The result? I often felt scattered, tense, emotionally ungrounded, and completely disconnected from my intuition.

But something shifted when I began treating my mornings as a vibrational practice, not just a productivity one.

That shift changed everything.

## THE FIRST 30 MINUTES MATTER

Your morning is not just the beginning of your day. It's the moment you set your frequency.

And the energy you begin with? It echoes.

It informs how you show up to your work. How you parent. How you create. How you make decisions.

If your morning begins with intention, your entire day becomes a reflection of that centered presence.

As women entrepreneurs, these first moments determine whether we'll lead from clarity or chaos, make decisions from wisdom or worry, and let our creativity flow or be blocked by mental noise.

Science backs this up.

When you wake, your brain is still moving through theta and alpha wave states—those dreamy, open frequencies that make your subconscious highly impressionable. This means that what you think, say, or focus on during this window carries extra weight.

You are, quite literally, programming your energy for the day.

Are you reinforcing survival states—rushing, comparing, stressing? Or are you aligning with the future version of you—the calm, grounded, embodied creator?

Your morning is your chance to choose.

## THE RITUAL THAT CHANGED EVERYTHING

One morning, after a particularly stressful stretch in my business, I tried something different.

Instead of reaching for my phone, I sat in bed with one hand on my heart and one on my belly.

I breathed. I asked myself: *How am I feeling?* I didn't try to fix anything—I just witnessed what was there.

And then I asked: *What do I want to feel today?*

That tiny moment—no more than five minutes—recalibrated everything. It brought me back into coherence. Back into me.

From that day forward, I began experimenting with simple, soulful rituals that helped me start my day with presence rather than pressure.

This transition was about balancing feminine and masculine energies in my approach to business. Rather than immediately rushing into doing and achieving (masculine energy), I created space for being, feeling, and receiving (feminine energy) first. This seemingly small change had a significant impact on my leadership, creativity, and decision-making throughout the day.

## HOW MY PRACTICE EVOLVED: THE BEACH RITUAL

As these morning moments became more sacred to me, I felt drawn to expand them. What began as a simple breathing practice evolved into something more immersive when I discovered the power of starting my day in nature.

Initially, it was just sunrise walks on the beach. There was something transformative about feeling the cool sand beneath my feet and watching the first light spill across the water. Just grounding brought me back to myself—calming my system and restoring clarity.Over time, this practice naturally expanded.

I began bringing my journal, capturing insights that seemed to flow more easily in this quieter space. I added reading—absorbing wisdom before the world's noise could crowd it out.

Eventually, even on winter mornings, I incorporated ocean swimming—that bracing cold becoming a full-body reset that awakened every cell.

This wasn't an elaborate plan I designed.

It was an organic evolution that followed what my body and spirit craved. Each element added another layer of presence, another way to connect with myself before connecting with the world.

The practice wasn't about perfectionism or productivity—it was about creating a container where my authentic self could emerge. These morning moments became the foundation upon which everything else in my day was built.

## SUNRISE VIEWING: THE MEDICINE OF MORNING LIGHT

One of the most restorative morning practices I've discovered wasn't something I needed to learn or perfect—it was simply showing up for what nature already offers us: the sunrise.

When I began my beach ritual, I was initially drawn to the peace and grounding of walking on sand. But over time, I realized something else was happening. The early morning light was actually resetting my entire system—my energy, focus, mood, and even my cellular function.

This wasn't just a nice experience.

It was medicine.

The science behind this is fascinating. When you witness the sunrise, you're exposing yourself to a unique quality of light that's gentler and more diffuse than at any other time of day. This early sunlight passes through more of the Earth's atmosphere, creating a perfect balance—enough light to trigger crucial biological processes, but not so intense that it causes damage.

Your eyes have special photoreceptors that don't just help you see. They help set your entire biological clock.

That first light of day sends signals to your brain to stop producing melatonin (the sleep hormone) and start releasing cortisol and other hormones that naturally energize you.

But there's something even more extraordinary happening. Morning sunlight exposure:

- **Resets your circadian rhythm**—synchronizing every system in your body with the natural day-night cycle
- **Boosts serotonin production**—improving your mood and emotional resilience throughout the day
- **Enhances ATP (adenosine triphosphate) production**—fueling your cells with energy to support focus, vitality, and overall cellular function
- **Supports natural vitamin D synthesis**—essential for immune function and bone health
- **Releases nitric oxide**—improving blood flow and cardiovascular health

I discovered something interesting, too: wearing sunglasses in the early morning actually blocks these benefits. While sun protection is important during peak hours, those first gentle rays need direct access to your eyes to work their magic.

This practice couldn't be simpler:

- Step outside within the first hour of sunrise.
- Face the direction of the rising sun.
- Spend just 5-10 minutes receiving this light (no sunglasses).
- Let your eyes gently take in the surrounding light. You don't need to stare directly at the sun, especially once it's risen above the horizon.

The energetic shift is palpable. There's a reason so many spiritual traditions honor the sunrise as a sacred time. It's a moment of pure potential—the beginning of a new cycle, a fresh start, a literal illumination.

For entrepreneurs especially, this practice grounds you in something larger than your business challenges. It reminds you that each day is a new beginning, that cycles of renewal are built into the very fabric of our world.

And on a practical level? I've found no better way to naturally wake up, focus my mind, and set my energy for a productive day than this simple act of showing up for the sun.

## THE RITUAL DOESN'T NEED TO BE PERFECT

You don't need an hour of silence and a sunrise meditation to claim your mornings. You just need a few intentional moments to align your energy before the world comes in.

Here are some of my favourite practices (choose one or layer them up):

- **Stillness or breathwork (2–5 minutes):** Even a few deep belly breaths can change your state
- **Journaling:** A stream-of-consciousness brain dump, or prompts like *"What do I need today?"*
- **Visualisation:** See yourself embodying your highest self—in business, in conversations, in confidence
- **Movement:** Gentle stretching, shaking, or a quick intuitive dance
- **Intention setting:** Speak it out loud: *"Today, I lead from calm clarity."*
- **Energy clearing:** A light sweep of your body with your hands or visual light

- **Silence:** Just sit with yourself, uninterrupted

None of this needs to be complex. It just needs to be consistent.

## FOR THE MOTHERS: SACRED MOMENTS IN THE MIDST OF CHAOS

If you're a mother with young children, I see you. The idea of uninterrupted morning time might feel like a fantasy from another lifetime. The moment your eyes open, little ones may already be calling your name.

But sacred morning time isn't about duration or perfection—it's about intention.

Perhaps your ritual is three deep breaths while your feet first touch the floor. Maybe it's a whispered intention while the shower water runs over you. Or a moment of connection while your coffee brews, before little voices need your attention.

A mother in my community keeps a journal by her bed and writes three lines before rising—what she feels, what she needs, and one thing she's calling in that day. Another sets her alarm just 10 minutes before her children typically wake, creating a tiny pocket of stillness.

The key isn't creating an elaborate practice—it's claiming even the smallest moment as yours. One conscious breath can do more than an hour of distracted meditation.

## BUT I'M NOT A MORNING PERSON...

That's okay. Truly.

This isn't about waking up at 5 a.m. or doing a full wellness circuit before sunrise.

It's about creating a moment of energetic sovereignty—whenever your day begins.

Whether it's after school drop-off, post-coffee, or even in your parked car before a meeting... You can create a window to return to yourself.

It's not the time that matters. It's the intention.

---

## 🌀 TRY THIS: CREATE YOUR 10-MINUTE MORNING FLOW

Here's a simple template to begin with:

1. **Ground**: Breathe or sit in stillness (2–3 minutes)
2. **Tune In**: Ask: *"How do I feel?"* + *"What do I need?"* (3–5 minutes journaling)
3. **Rise**: Speak your intention, visualize your energy expanding, or move your body (2–5 minutes)

You can do all of this before you leave the bedroom. Before emails. Before the kids. Before the outside world gets a say.

For entrepreneurs, this practice becomes the foundation for inspired action rather than reactive hustle. The decisions you make, the content you create, the way you show up for your team and clients—all of it flows from this centered place of clarity.

---

## THE RIPPLE EFFECT: HOW MORNING RITUALS TRANSFORM YOUR BUSINESS DAY

When I began consistently practicing these morning rituals, I noticed meaningful changes that carried through the rest of my day—and beyond:

**Clearer decision-making:** By starting with grounded presence rather than reactivity, I found myself making business decisions from intuition rather than fear. The mental noise cleared, and the right path forward often revealed itself without the struggle I'd previously experienced.

**Enhanced creativity:** Those morning moments of receptivity opened channels for inspiration that persisted throughout the day. Content ideas, program structures, and solutions to client challenges would appear seemingly out of nowhere—because I'd created the space for them to emerge.

**Increased resilience:** The emotional regulation that began in my morning practice extended into challenging moments. When a launch didn't go as planned or difficult feedback arrived, I could respond from my center rather than spiral into anxiety or doubt.

**Magnetic presence:** I noticed that client calls and team interactions flowed differently. I was fully present rather than scattered, which created a container where others felt truly seen and heard. This directly translated into increased client retention, enhanced team trust, and more effective leadership.

**Energy sustainability:** Perhaps most importantly, these morning moments helped me break the cycle of depletion that had characterized my earlier business journey. By starting with filling my cup, I had more genuine energy to pour into my work without the afternoon crashes or end-of-week exhaustion.

I watched these same benefits unfold for clients who implemented their own morning rituals. One found that her sales conversations became significantly more successful—not because she changed her offers, but because she changed the energy she brought to those calls. Another reported that her content creation became effortless after years of writer's block simply because she began her workday from a different vibrational state.

This isn't magical thinking—it's energetic coherence in action. The frequency you establish in those first moments creates the container for everything that follows.

## CLOSING: START AS YOU INTEND TO CONTINUE

The way you start your day teaches your nervous system how to show up in the world.

It's a frequency setting. A recalibration. A declaration.

You're not just starting your day, you're anchoring who you are becoming.

So tomorrow, before the world floods in, take a moment to flood yourself first—with breath, with presence, with power.

Start your day as the woman you're rising into.

And then... continue as her.

# CHAPTER 12
# DAILY PRACTICES DAILY PRACTICES THAT ANCHOR AND ELEVATE YOU

YOUR VIBRATION ISN'T SET and forget.

It's something you return to. Choose again. Stabilize. Realign.

These aren't just morning rituals. They're tools you can call on throughout your day—especially when the world gets loud, your thoughts get busy, or your energy begins to contract.

In the last chapter, I shared how meditation and gratitude journaling became part of my morning rhythm. But over time, I discovered that these practices were even more powerful when I integrated them into my day.

They became gentle anchors, small but potent moments of re-alignment—not just a "nice idea" but an energetic necessity.

And the more I integrated them, the more I noticed something else...

They were balancing something deeper inside me.

A subtle shift. A quiet strength.

They were restoring the parts of me that had been overworked, overpushed, and overstretched.

These practices became a portal back into my feminine energy—and my full presence.

## VIBRATIONAL HEALTH = ENERGETIC RESILIENCE

You can think of vibrational health as your emotional immune system.

When it's strong, you recover faster from stress. You move through discomfort without shutting down. You stay anchored in your power, even when the day doesn't go to plan.

These practices—meditation, gratitude, breathwork—are not just for calm mornings and self-care Sundays.

They are your tools for staying coherent in the messy middle of life and business.

As entrepreneurs, we face unique vibrational challenges. Client disappointments, technology breakdowns, cash flow concerns. These aren't just practical issues, they're energetic ones. Each has the power to pull us out of our center and into reactive patterns that drain our creativity and cloud our vision.

What if, instead of being thrown by these moments, you had the tools to stay anchored? To respond from wisdom rather than reaction? This is the power of vibrational health practices woven throughout your day.

## PRACTICE 1: MEDITATION

### A Moment to Return to You

Let's bust a myth right now: You don't need to sit in silence for 30 minutes and clear your mind.

Meditation is not about "doing it right." It's about coming home to yourself.

Sometimes, that looks like:

- Sitting for 5 minutes with one hand on your heart
- Following your breath as you walk or lie down
- Listening to a guided track while you take a break from your laptop

Personally, I've used everything from visualisation meditations to body scans and quantum field journeys. Some days I crave silence. Other days, I need a little support.

What matters is not the method—it's the moment you pause and reconnect.

For entrepreneurs, meditation becomes a high-impact business tool. I've watched client after client elevate their leadership presence, creative flow, and decision-making clarity through this practice. One particular client noticed that after implementing just 10 minutes of meditation before client calls, her close rate increased by 20%—not because she changed her offer, but because she changed the energy she brought to those conversations.

Science supports this understanding. A study conducted by researchers at Massachusetts General Hospital and Harvard Medical School, led by Britta K. Hölzel and Sara W. Lazar, demonstrated that participating in an eight-week Mindfulness-Based Stress Reduction (MBSR) program led to increases in gray matter density in brain regions associated with learning, memory, self-awareness, and compassion (Hölzel et al., 2011). These structural changes suggest that meditation not only influences our emotional state but also enhances brain function, which can be particularly beneficial during challenging business situations and creative endeavors.

If you're new to meditation or prefer support, you can find beautiful free resources on Spotify, YouTube, or apps like Insight Timer and Calm.

📌 *Tip: If you have more time for meditation, try Dr. Joe Dispenza's deep guided journeys.*

## PRACTICE 2: GRATITUDE

**The Fastest Way to Raise Your Vibration**

You've already heard this a thousand times. But the power of it never gets old:

Gratitude changes your vibration—instantly.

Why?

Because it pulls you out of fear, lack, comparison... and brings you into presence, fullness, enoughness.

It rewires your brain to scan for what's working. It softens your nervous system. It calls your energy back into your body.

Through Hawkins' pioneering work measuring emotional frequencies, we learned something signifcant: gratitude registers at a significantly higher vibration than most emotions, sitting near 540—a powerful bridge between the lower states of consciousness and the higher realms of joy, peace, and enlightenment.

This isn't just spiritual teaching, it's quantifiable, energetic science. When you consciously choose gratitude, you're literally moving yourself up the vibrational scale—from lower-frequency emotional states into higher ones. This elevation impacts everything from your physical health to your creative capacity and intuitive access.

This doesn't mean you need to write a novel every day.

Some of my most effective gratitude practices have been the simplest:

*"I'm grateful for this cup of tea."*
*"I'm grateful I gave myself a moment to pause."*
*"I'm grateful for my own courage today."*

What matters is the emotion behind it. Feel it. Let it land in your body.

In business, gratitude becomes a strategic advantage. When you constantly scan for what's working—the client wins, the small breakthroughs, the lessons in challenges—you operate at a completely different frequency than most entrepreneurs, who remain fixated on gaps and problems.

Want to supercharge it?

***Try Gratitude Stacking:*** Throughout the day, stack tiny moments of joy and gratitude—and name them out loud. This creates a compounding energetic effect.

## PRACTICE 3: BREATHWORK

**Your Built-In Reset Button**

Breath is the most accessible healing tool you have. It's free. It's fast. It's always with you.

And it's one of the most effective ways to realign your energetic state.

Whether you're feeling anxious, scattered, overwhelmed, or over-stimulated, conscious breathing will bring you back into coherence.

For women, especially, breathwork creates an immediate pathway from the sympathetic nervous system (fight-or-flight) to the parasympathetic state (rest-and-digest). This is crucial because our best ideas, clearest intuition, and most aligned decisions emerge from this calmer state.

I remember preparing for a high-stakes investor meeting that had my stomach in knots. Five minutes of coherent breathing moved me from anxiety to grounded confidence. That meeting secured the funding that allowed me to expand my business into what it is today —all because I had the tools to change my energy before walking into the room.

Here are a few practices I use and recommend to my clients:

- **Box Breathing:** Inhale 4 → Hold 4 → Exhale 4 → Hold 4
- **4-7-8:** Inhale for 4 → Hold for 7 → Exhale for 8
- **Sighing:** Inhale deeply, then sigh out through your mouth. Repeat 3–5 times
- **Coherence Breathing:** Inhale for 5 → Exhale for 5 (through the nose)

It takes as little as 60 seconds to feel the difference ripple through your body.

Some days, I'll pause in the middle of a workday, lie down, and breathe. Just to reset. Just to come back.

If you're more audio-driven, look up "guided breathwork" on YouTube or Spotify. I personally love the Soma Breathwork "Morning Gratitude" session—it's a beautiful combination of breathwork and gratitude practice that energizes and centers me in under 15 minutes.

## PRACTICE 4: NON-SLEEP DEEP REST (NSDR)

Throughout your day, your energy can easily scatter—whether through stress, decision fatigue, or the natural demands of entrepreneurship. One powerful way to recalibrate and restore your vibrational state is through Non-Sleep Deep Rest (NSDR).

Popularized by neuroscientist Dr. Andrew Huberman, NSDR involves consciously relaxing your body while staying mentally aware, allowing your brain to access deep recovery states without needing to fall asleep.

Even a short NSDR session can boost your dopamine levels, enhance neuroplasticity, and leave you feeling clearer, calmer, and more focused.

It's one more reminder that vibrational leadership isn't just about pushing through — it's about learning to pause, replenish, and realign, even in the small spaces between tasks.

## THE FEMININE POWER OF INTEGRATION

What makes these practices particularly potent is how they reconnect us to our feminine essence—the receptive, intuitive, and cyclical nature that is often overshadowed in traditional business environments.

The masculine energy of business drives us toward constant action, linear thinking, and perseverance. These practices balance that drive by creating moments of receptivity, cyclical awareness, and inner connection.

This isn't about rejecting action or achievement. It's about ensuring they flow from a centered place rather than anxious striving.

When I speak with women in my programs about their most significant business breakthroughs, they rarely mention hustling harder. Instead, they talk about the moment they finally slowed down enough to hear their intuition. The afternoon meditation that revealed a completely new program idea. The gratitude practice that transformed their relationship with money.

These aren't coincidences. They're what happens when we create space for feminine wisdom to emerge alongside our masculine drive.

## MAKING IT REAL: INTEGRATION THROUGHOUT YOUR DAY

The biggest objection I hear is: *"But I don't have time for this."*

I get it. Your calendar is packed. You're juggling multiple roles and responsibilities—and I've been there too. There was a time when just the thought of adding *one more thing* to my day felt impossible.

But here's what I discovered: the more I tried to push through and do it all, the more depleted and disconnected I became.

It wasn't until self-love became part of my daily foundation—not a luxury or add-on—that real transformation took root. These moments of pause and presence didn't slow me down. They actually made me more focused, more grounded, and more productive. I stopped operating on fumes and started showing up as the version of myself that could lead, create, and perform at my best—without burning out.

That's why this work matters. It's not about adding pressure. It's about building a foundation that sustains you.

Here's how I approach it and encourage my clients to as well:

**Anchor to existing habits:** Pair these practices with things you already do. Meditate while your coffee brews. Practice gratitude in the shower. Do breathwork at stoplights or while waiting for Zoom calls to start.

**Create micro-moments:** Not every practice needs to take 20 minutes. Sometimes, a 60-second breath reset or a 2-minute gratitude pause is enough to reset your nervous system, elevate your energy, and reconnect you with your centre.

**Use transitions wisely:** The spaces between activities are perfect for these practices. Before opening your laptop, after closing a call, between client sessions—these transition moments are portals for realignment.

**Make it visible:** Keep visual reminders in your workspace. A small stone that represents presence. A sticky note with "Breathe" on your computer. A gratitude prompt as your phone background.

The most sustainable approach is the one that fits your real life—not an idealized version of it.

---

## ◎ TRY THIS: CHOOSE YOUR ANCHOR

What do you most need today?

Stillness to return to yourself?

Gratitude to lift your emotional state?

Breathwork to calm and reset?

Choose just one. Let it be your anchor—your moment to return, to soften, to align.

Notice how this single practice impacts not just how you feel but how you show up in your business. What becomes possible when you operate from this more aligned state?

---

## OPTIONAL SUPPORT: A CURATED PLAYLIST

To make things easy, I've created a playlist on YouTube with some of my favorites:

- Guided meditations
- Breathwork tracks
- Morning activations

- Calming evening audio
- High-vibe soundscapes

📱 You can access the playlist by scanning the QR code (Figure 12.1).

Figure 12.1

## CLOSING: REGULATE TO RISE

You don't need a perfect routine. You need a way to come back to your body. Your frequency. Your power.

The more often you return to your center, the stronger your vibrational baseline becomes. These practices don't just support your energy—they support your leadership. Your intuition. Your capacity to serve, build, and rise.

Regulate your nervous system... And watch how much easier it is to receive what you've been calling in.

## CHAPTER 13
# NOURISHING YOUR MIND: HOW INTENTIONAL MENTAL INPUT SHAPES YOUR BUSINESS OUTPUT

TRUE GROWTH BEGINS the moment we begin to nourish our mind intentionally—when we start choosing what we read and listen to not just for entertainment or education, but as a way to grow into the next version of ourselves.

This isn't about "doing more." It's about feeding your mind the way you feed your body—with care, discernment, and intention.

Because what you consume? Becomes your energy. Becomes your beliefs. Becomes your identity.

## YOUR MENTAL DIET SHAPES YOUR EXPANSION

You might not always be able to control what happens externally, but you can choose what you allow to shape your inner world.

For years, I told myself I wasn't really a reader.

*"I'm too busy."*
*"I don't have time."*
*"I'll never finish a whole book."*

But when I finally paused to question that belief, I realized it wasn't true. It was just a program—one that had been running beneath the surface and keeping me from a deeply nourishing practice.

Since then, I've learned that both reading and intentional listening are forms of energetic hygiene. They recalibrate your thoughts, stretch your perspective, and strengthen your connection to the identity you're stepping into.

## BECOMING A READER (EVEN IF YOU THINK YOU'RE NOT)

If the idea of reading feels overwhelming, I hear you.

Start small.

Pick up a book that speaks to you, and allow your intuition to guide your choice. Some of the most meaningful growth I've experienced has come from books that "called me" at the exact moment I needed them—even when I didn't know why.

Sometimes, you don't need a whole book. You need one chapter. One paragraph. One sentence. The kind that lands in your body and doesn't leave.

Reading a physical book invites a deeper kind of presence.

The weight of the pages in your hand.
The act of underlining or highlighting a line that hits deep.
Writing notes in the margins.
Returning to passages again and again.

These rituals, small and seemingly insignificant, become portals of reflection.

And there's neuroscience behind it, too. Research shows that when you physically engage with a book—by underlining, circling, or annotating—you activate the brain's **motor memory system**, which strengthens neural encoding and improves retention. This embodied interaction helps the content stick not just in your mind, but in your lived experience.

This is how wisdom moves from the page into your bones.

## READING RITUALS THAT ANCHOR YOU

You don't need a strict reading schedule. But weaving it into your day as a sacred moment of reset can help you ground, refocus, and realign with the person you're becoming.

Try:

- A few pages with your morning tea
- Ten minutes while you wait in the car
- A chapter to unwind before bed
- A mid-day break to shift your focus and energy
- Over time, these moments become more than a habit. They become anchors.

## READING → REFLECTION → INTEGRATION

What reading has taught me most is that growth doesn't end with the last sentence—it begins when we live it.

Often, what I've read stirs something in me that leads to journaling, meditation, or even emotional release.

You might want to keep a "growth journal" nearby as you read—a space to jot down quotes, insights, or questions that arise. These reflections often deepen your integration of the material and help you apply it in real time.

Sometimes the book is the teacher. Sometimes, it's what the book activates in you.

## LISTENING WITH INTENTION: THE POWER OF PODCASTS

While books are grounding, podcasts are portable power sources—perfect for moments when you're walking, driving, cooking, or between appointments.

But here's the key: don't just listen passively. Let your listening become a practice.

When you hear something that resonates, pause. Jot it down. Reflect on it. Ask yourself: How does this apply to my life or business right now?

Podcasts can often spark the same kind of growth as reading, especially when you engage with them actively.

Here's how to deepen the impact of what you listen to:

1. **Take Notes:** Keep a small notebook or open your Notes app. Capture phrases, ideas, or reframes that strike a chord.
2. **Reflect and Apply:** Use what you've noted as journaling prompts or discussion starters. Let the content evolve from inspiration into embodiment.
3. **Share the Insight:** Talk about what you've learned with a friend, mentor, or mastermind group. This not only reinforces your understanding, but it also attracts aligned conversations and deepens the connection.

Podcasts become impactful when they don't just entertain you—they help expand you.

## ◎ TRY THIS: CREATE YOUR PERSONAL GROWTH FLOW

Here's a simple practice:

- Choose one book to explore this month
- Choose one podcast that aligns with your current season
- Decide on a simple reading/listening window (10 minutes/day is enough)
- Keep a journal or Notes doc to track insights, quotes, and "ah-ha" moments

Over time, this becomes a library of evolution—a living record of your becoming.

---

## PERSONAL GROWTH AS BUSINESS STRATEGY

What's fascinating about intentional reading and listening is how deeply it impacts your business—even when the content isn't explicitly "business-focused."

My most significant breakthroughs as an entrepreneur haven't always come from business strategy books or marketing podcasts. Often, they've emerged from consuming content about:

- Personal development
- Spiritual growth
- Psychology and human behavior
- Mindfulness and presence

Why? Because business challenges are rarely just about tactics or strategies.

They're about how you:

- Navigate uncertainty
- Process emotions when things get hard
- Make decisions when there's no clear answer
- Stay centered during rapid growth or setbacks
- Access your intuition for creative solutions

The entrepreneur who reads widely develops an agility of mind that tactical knowledge alone cannot provide.

When I faced a significant decision about expanding my business, it wasn't a business book that helped me find clarity. It was a book on intuitive decision-making that gave me the framework to trust myself. When dealing with complex client situations, my ability to remain grounded came directly from my morning reading practice on presence and emotional intelligence.

These "non-business" inputs create the internal environment from which your best business decisions flow. They expand your capacity to handle complexity, navigate relationships, and stay connected to your purpose when challenges arise.

Your business can only grow to the extent that you do. And intentional reading and listening are among the most effective catalysts for that growth.

---

## 🌀 TRY THIS: ALIGN YOUR INPUTS WITH YOUR IDENTITY

Ask yourself:

*What am I currently reading or listening to?*
*Is it aligned with the woman I'm becoming?*

*What's one new piece of content I can commit to this week that supports my next level?*

Write it down. Commit to it. Let it nourish your growth.

---

## CLOSING REFLECTION: THE ENTREPRENEUR'S MIND AS SACRED GROUND

What we allow into our minds shapes everything: our decisions, our energy, our capacity to innovate and lead.

As entrepreneurs, our minds are our most valuable assets. What we feed them determines what we can create, how we can serve, and who we can become.

When you move from random consumption to intentional nourishment, you're making a clear declaration about your commitment to growth—not just as a business owner, but as the visionary behind your work.

This isn't about perfectionism or cramming more into your already-full days. It's about honoring your evolution with the same care and intention you bring to your business strategy.

The breakthroughs your business and life are craving may be tucked inside a book, spoken through a podcast, or revealed in a moment of stillness.

Your next level of thinking—and, therefore your next level of business—begins with what you choose to let in.

Choose wisely. Choose intentionally. Choose what helps you rise.

# CHAPTER 14
# MINDFUL MEDIA CONSUMPTION: CURATING INPUT TO PROTECT YOUR ENERGY AND FOCUS

YOU'VE JUST CHOSEN to feed your mind with intention—through books, podcasts, and inspiring voices that elevate your growth.

Now it's time to look at the other side of the coin.

Because for everything we consciously choose to consume, there's an avalanche of content we passively absorb.

Emails. News alerts. Social media. Scrolling while tired. Comparison loops that sneak in when we're just "checking in."

And here's the truth:

**What you consume in the background still imprints your energy.**

It still shapes your nervous system. It still affects your thoughts, your mood, and your beliefs.

## WHEN MY PHONE BECAME A FREQUENCY THIEF

I noticed something strange happening.

I'd start my mornings in complete alignment—intentions set, meditation complete, priorities clear. My energy would be high. Ideas flowing. Purpose radiating through me.

But by 2 p.m.? Something unraveled.

My focus scattered.
My energy drained.
That sense of clarity... gone.

For weeks, I couldn't figure out what was happening. Until I caught myself one day.

There I was, reaching for my phone... again. Not for any real reason. Just habit.

What started as "just checking messages" would spiral into:

- A "quick" scroll through Instagram.
- News headlines about crises I couldn't solve.
- Comment threads that pulled me deeper.
- A little game when a project felt challenging.

I'd pick up my phone without even knowing why—then find myself getting a hit of digital dopamine.

The moment it all clicked was during a creative project that required my complete presence. I hit a challenging point—that moment when creation gets uncomfortable. And before my conscious mind even registered it, my hand was reaching for my phone.

Pure habit. A programmed response to discomfort.

What I realized changed everything: these innocent "breaks" were actually frequency disruptors.

Fear-based headlines. Subtle comparison triggers. Even mindless games.

All of it was pulling me out of my higher frequency state and into something... lower.

And here's where I had to get honest with myself. As we explored earlier through Hawkins' *Scale of Consciousness*, emotions like fear, anger, shame, and guilt sit at the very bottom of the vibrational spectrum. They're not just passing feelings—they're energetic states.

So every time I absorbed content saturated in those frequencies, I was feeding my mind low-vibration energy. And because energy is always influencing energy, my own state would begin to match that input. Not just mentally, but energetically.

I wasn't just consuming content—I was being conditioned by it.

And it wasn't just my daytime habits.

Night after night, I'd collapse on the couch, open Netflix, and mindlessly watch reality TV or series with heavy, dramatic themes. Shows filled with conflict, tension, and fear.

I'd think I was "relaxing." But my body was absorbing every bit of that energy. I'd go to bed feeling tense. Heavy. My mind racing with stories that weren't even mine.

As my awareness of my energy grew, these disruptions became impossible to ignore. I wasn't just losing time—I was losing the energetic momentum I'd worked so hard to build.

Here's what surprised me most: once I created boundaries around these habits, I didn't miss them at all.

I still check the news once a day. I still use social media for specific purposes. I still watch movies and shows—but now I choose ones that make me laugh, share inspirational stories, or help me grow personally, like the content on Gaia TV.

The difference in my creative output, decision clarity, and well-being has been significant.

This isn't about perfection or disconnecting from the world—it's about reclaiming energetic sovereignty.

It's not that I never use these platforms. It's that I now decide *when*, *how*, and *why* I engage.

And that conscious choice changes everything.

Because here's what I came to understand:

**Your attention is energetic currency.**

In a world designed to hijack it, choosing what you *don't* consume is just as important as what you do.

We often think of boundaries in terms of relationships—what we allow from others, what we say yes or no to.

But one of the most important boundaries you can create is with your inputs.

Who gets to speak into your mind?
Whose energy are you letting in through your screen?
What kinds of stories are shaping your internal world, just because you scroll past them every day?

By trading unconscious scrolling for intentional engagement, you begin to stabilize your frequency.

You begin to hear your own thoughts again. You come home to yourself.

## HIGH INPUT, LOW ALIGNMENT

Here's how you'll often know your digital hygiene needs an upgrade:

- You feel drained after being online, even if nothing "bad" happened
- You start your day with the news and immediately feel anxious
- You catch yourself comparing your life, business, or body to strangers
- You find yourself doom-scrolling when you're stressed or numb
- You open Instagram to "relax" and leave feeling tight in your chest

This isn't weakness. It's overstimulation.

Your nervous system is absorbing energy at a rate it hasn't evolved to process. And if you don't take the reins… someone else will.

## THE ENTREPRENEURIAL COST OF DIGITAL DISTRACTION

As business owners, we face a unique challenge with digital consumption. While everyone experiences the personal impacts of mindless scrolling or negative content, entrepreneurs face additional consequences:

**Decision Fatigue:** Every piece of content you consume requires a micro-decision from your brain. By mid-afternoon, your decision-making capacity for important business choices can be depleted by hundreds of inconsequential digital decisions.

**Creative Depletion:** The constant influx of others' ideas, opinions, and content can overwhelm your own creative voice. Many entrepreneurs find that their most innovative solutions emerge during periods of digital minimalism.

**Comparison Spiral:** Nothing kills entrepreneurial confidence faster than the highlight reels of others' success. What started as "market research" can quickly become a self-doubt trigger that impacts your pricing, offerings, and brand voice.

**Energy Misalignment:** Building a business requires substantial energetic investment. Every moment spent in low-vibrational digital spaces is energy diverted from your vision, clients, and growth.

The most successful entrepreneurs I know aren't necessarily disconnected from digital media—they're simply intentional about it. They recognize that their creativity, decision-making capability, and energetic presence are business assets worth protecting.

---

## ⊚ TRY THIS: YOUR 7-DAY DIGITAL RESET

Let's reshape the way you engage with digital content—through a structured blend of awareness, intention, and aligned action:

**Step 1: Audit Your Current Patterns (Days 1-2)**

Start by noticing what's currently happening:

- Track when you feel compelled to check your phone
- Notice which apps you open first by default
- Observe how you feel before and after digital consumption
- Ask yourself these deeper questions:
    - Which accounts consistently leave you feeling inspired vs. depleted?
    - When are you most likely to fall into passive scrolling?

- What emotions trigger unconscious digital consumption?
- How does your current consumption support or hinder your business goals?

**Step 2: Clear and Curate (Day 3-4)**

Now that you're aware, it's time to consciously redesign your digital environment:

- Unfollow or mute accounts that drain your energy
- Adjust your feed settings to prioritize uplifting content
- Clear out notification settings that pull your attention
- Choose what to add:
    - Follow accounts that educate, inspire, or uplift
    - Subscribe to newsletters or blogs from aligned mentors
    - Set up digital spaces that reflect the woman you're becoming

**Step 3: Create Intentional Boundaries (Days 5-7)**

Establish clear structures to maintain your energetic sovereignty:

- Set specific times for checking email (e.g., 10 a.m. and 3 p.m. only)
- Designate "phone-free zones" (first hour after waking, meals, before bed)
- Create alternative rituals for when you feel the urge to scroll:
    - Three deep breaths
    - A quick stretch
    - Jotting down a thought or idea
    - Drinking a glass of water
    - Looking out the window for 30 seconds

**Step 4: Balance Business Use**

For the social media you need for business:

- Schedule specific times for business-related social media tasks
- Consider separating business accounts from personal browsing
- Create a rule to share your own content before consuming others' content
- Before opening any platform, take three deep breaths and set a clear intention

<u>Remember</u>: You don't need a complete digital detox. You just need to return to choice.

**Step 5: Reflect and Evolve**

After your 7-day reset, take time to notice:

- What changes did you observe in your energy and creativity?
- Which new habits felt sustainable?
- What boundaries will you maintain moving forward?

This isn't about perfection—it's about interrupting unconscious patterns and creating space for your highest frequency to emerge.

---

## CLOSING REFLECTION: GUARD YOUR FREQUENCY LIKE GOLD

In this season of becoming, your energy is your most valuable asset.

So guard it. Curate it. Choose what gets access to your mind and nervous system.

Every scroll, every click, every headline... is either supporting your expansion or feeding your contraction.

You're not just here to "manage" your attention. You're here to reclaim your energetic sovereignty.

Let your digital environment become a sanctuary for growth—not a drain on your power.

Because a regulated, discerning woman?

**She's unstoppable.**

# CHAPTER 15
# FROM BODY TO BUSINESS: PHYSICAL RITUALS THAT FUEL VIBRATIONAL RESILIENCE

THERE'S a moment when all the mindset work in the world isn't enough.

You've journaled. You've meditated. You've tried reframing your thoughts. But the energy still feels stuck.

That's when you remember... Your body isn't just carrying your energy. It is energy.

And it's asking to move. To ground. To reset.

Because your physical body is one of the most effective tools you have for regulating and raising your vibrational state.

## THE BODY AS FREQUENCY STABILIZER

As we explored in the morning routine chapter, my beach ritual became an integration of multiple practices. What began as time for journaling, reading, and meditation naturally expanded to include movement, grounding, and cold therapy.

Those mornings on the beach allowed me to combine so many elements in one beautiful experience—my bare feet in the sand, the ocean swim, and walking along the shore. It became more than just a routine; it was a source of tremendous joy and gratitude, a way to address my mind, body, and spirit all at once.

But even if you don't live near a beach, the principle remains the same:

Vibrational health is a full-body practice.

Your nervous system stores your stories. Your fascia holds your fears. Your cells record your state.

If energy is not allowed to move through, it gets stuck. And when it gets stuck? You feel foggy, anxious, reactive, and drained—no matter how much "inner work" you do.

This chapter is about clearing that energy. Physically. Gently. Intentionally.

## GROUNDING: RECONNECT TO REGULATE

We touched on this in your morning rituals—that simple act of placing your feet on the earth, touching a tree, or sitting in nature.

It may sound too simple to matter, but it's one of the most potent vibrational reset tools available.

Grounding, also known as earthing, refers to making direct skin contact with the Earth's surface. Scientifically, this allows your body to absorb negatively charged electrons, which help neutralize free radicals and reduce inflammation.

And energetically? It anchors your spirit into the now.

In our modern world of EMFs, concrete, synthetic flooring, rubbersouled shoes, and screen time, we've become physically and energetically disconnected from the Earth.

But your body remembers.

The first time I intentionally grounded during burnout, I took off my shoes and slowly walked across the grass. The tension in my shoulders softened. My thoughts slowed. My breath deepened.

It felt like I had returned to myself.

Ways to ground:

- Barefoot walks on grass, sand, or soil
- Sitting with your back against a tree
- Placing your hands in water, dirt, or the ocean
- Using a grounding mat indoors

Even 5 minutes makes a difference, especially between meetings or during a creative block.

## THE ENTREPRENEUR'S GROUNDING PRACTICE

As business owners, we spend our days in our heads. Strategy. Planning. Content. Decisions.

It's a recipe for disconnection.

I remember a day I had three client calls back-to-back, followed by a team meeting during which we made significant decisions about our next launch.

By 2 p.m., my thoughts were scattered, my energy felt chaotic, and my ability to make clear decisions had vanished.

Instead of pushing through (my old pattern), I stepped outside. No phone. No shoes. Just 7 minutes with my feet on the grass.

When I returned to my desk, everything felt different. The launch decisions that felt overwhelming became clear. The creative block I'd been experiencing dissolved. My energy had reset.

This wasn't coincidence.

Research shows that grounding reduces cortisol (your stress hormone) and improves heart rate variability (a key measure of nervous system balance). For us as entrepreneurs, this translates directly to clearer decision-making and enhanced creative flow.

Even in the busiest seasons, you can integrate grounding:

- Between Zoom calls, step outside for 3 minutes
- Take client calls while walking barefoot in your garden
- Start team meetings with a 2-minute earthing practice
- Keep a grounding mat under your desk for all-day connection

The most successful entrepreneurs I know aren't just strategic with their time—they're intentional with their energy. And grounding is one of the simplest ways to stabilize and elevate your frequency, especially during pivotal business moments.

## GENTLE MOVEMENT: FEMININE ENERGY IN MOTION

We've been raised in a culture that glorifies masculine movement: high intensity, pushing harder, no days off.

But if you're already operating in masculine energy all day—leading, achieving, doing—then adding a punishing workout may actually deplete your frequency, not raise it.

That's why gentle movement is so essential to feminine energy balance.

It doesn't mean you can't lift weights or go for a run. But you also need space to move intuitively. To stretch. To sway. To breathe as you move—not just grit your way through it.

We're talking about movement that releases energy, not burns calories. That reconnects you to your body, not punishes it.

For years, I thought movement had to be hard to count. Now? It's about how it feels. How it flows. How it returns me to myself.

## MOVEMENT AS BUSINESS MEDICINE

I used to think I didn't have time to move during my workday. Too many emails. Too many deliverables. Too many responsibilities.

Until I noticed a pattern...

The days I skipped movement were the days my creativity tanked. My patience thinned. My ability to see possibilities narrowed.

Movement isn't a luxury for entrepreneurs—it's a necessity.

Especially feminine-aligned movement that allows energy to flow rather than forcing it to perform.

The turning point came during a launch that wasn't gaining traction. I'd been sitting at my computer for days, trying to "figure it out." The more I pushed, the more stuck everything felt.

One afternoon, instead of another strategy session, I put on music and allowed myself to dance. No structure. No goal. Just pure, intuitive movement.

Twenty minutes later, I returned to my desk, and the solution I'd been searching for appeared effortlessly. The launch messaging realigned, and everything started flowing.

This wasn't magic—it was neuroscience. Movement increases circulation to your brain, releases creativity-enhancing endorphins, and activates different neural pathways than those associated with linear thinking.

For women entrepreneurs, especially, our power comes through flow, not force.

Try integrating movement into your business day:

- A 5-minute stretch between calls
- A dance break when you hit a creative block
- A walking meeting (alone or with the team)
- Gentle yoga poses while problem-solving

You'll discover that the answers you've been seeking often emerge not through more thinking but through allowing your body to lead.

Your body isn't separate from your business genius—it's the vessel that carries it.

## COLD THERAPY: STRENGTHENING THE NERVOUS SYSTEM

Have you ever ended a shower with 30 seconds of cold water?

The first time I did, I gasped... fought it... But after reading the research, I knew this practice was important. A few days later, I did it again. A few seconds longer. Then again. And again.

And slowly, a new kind of strength emerged—not just physically, but emotionally.

Cold therapy is a high-impact practice for building nervous system resilience—and as an entrepreneur, that's gold.

When you train your body to breathe through discomfort—rather than resist it—you become stronger in every area of life.

Business challenges. Feedback. Pivots. High-stress decisions. You meet them differently when your system knows how to stay calm under pressure.

The science behind cold therapy? It's pretty mind-blowing.

When that cold water hits your skin, it activates your vagus nerve – that's the superhighway of your "rest and digest" nervous system (VagusNerve.com, n.d.). Your body releases norepinephrine (think clarity, focus, and mood elevation in a bottle) (Premier Sport Psychology, 2025). And at the cellular level? You're literally becoming more resilient, teaching every cell in your body how to handle stress better (ScienceDaily, 2025).

But here's something I discovered that changed everything for me: **women experience cold differently than men.**

Dr. Stacy Sims (2025), who's revolutionizing how we think about women's physiology, puts it bluntly: "Women are not small men." I love how she cuts through the noise in just a few words.

While everyone talks about ice baths and extreme cold plunges, Dr. Sims offers a game-changer for us women entrepreneurs – we don't need that kind of extreme cold to get the benefits! In fact, going too cold might actually stress our systems instead of strengthening them (Pippa Campbell Health, n.d.).

Here's what works for our unique female biology:

- Water around 15°C (59°F) – significantly warmer than what the guys are doing in all those studies (Sims, 2025)
- Start with shorter dips (even 30 seconds makes a difference!)
- Listen to YOUR body – not Instagram
- Try alternating between warm and cool (some women find this contrast approach gives them amazing energy and mood benefits)

This was a game changer for me. I didn't have to torture myself with ice-cold water to build resilience! My moderate-temperature cold showers and cold ocean swims became something I actually looked forward to rather than dreaded.

Remember, your unique female body has wisdom. Honor it.

## COLD EXPOSURE: YOUR LEADERSHIP EDGE

Business ownership will test you. Launch failures. Difficult clients. Team challenges. Financial pressure.

What separates sustainable success from burnout is how your nervous system responds to these inevitable stressors.

Cold therapy isn't just a wellness trend—it's entrepreneurial training.

When I first began practicing cold exposure, I noticed something fascinating. The voice in my head during those initial seconds of cold water—"*I can't do this, this is too much, make it stop*"—was the exact same voice I heard during business challenges.

By learning to breathe through the physical discomfort, I was rewiring my response to all forms of stress.

A client of mine, Sarah, incorporated a 60-second cold shower into her morning routine before launching her first high-ticket offer. She was terrified of rejection and criticism. But each morning, as she stood under that cold water, breathing steadily while her mind screamed to get out, she was practicing the exact skill she needed—staying regulated during discomfort.

Her launch was far from perfect. But instead of spiraling when things went wrong, she found herself responding with the same centered breath she'd cultivated in the cold.

The result? Her most successful offer to date, not because everything went right, but because she could navigate what went wrong.

Even 30 seconds of cold can open the doorway to nervous system recalibration and energetic reset. Start where you are, and build gradually. The goal isn't extremes—it's teaching your system to remain centered, even in the face of challenges.

Your business resilience begins with your biological resilience.

---

## 🌀 TRY THIS: YOUR PHYSICAL RESET PROTOCOL

**Step 1: Identify Your Current State**

Take a moment to check in with your energy:

- Where do you feel tension or constriction in your body?
- Does your energy feel scattered, depleted, or stagnant?
- What physical sensation would you most like to ease or transform?

**Step 2: Choose Your Practice**

Based on your current state, select one practice that feels most aligned:

For scattered energy or overthinking:

- 5 minutes of barefoot grounding
- Place one hand on your heart, one on your belly, and take 10 deep breaths
- Stand with your back against a tree for 3 minutes

For stagnant or stuck energy:

- 10 minutes of intuitive movement to music you love
- Gentle stretching focused on areas of tension
- A short walk with deliberate presence

For depleted energy or burnout signals:

- 30 seconds of cold water at the end of your shower
- Face immersion in cold water while holding breath for 15-30 seconds
- Alternate nostril breathing for 2 minutes

**Step 3: Implement Without Distraction**

- Put devices on "do not disturb"
- Set a timer if needed
- Commit to being fully present for this short practice

**Step 4: Notice the Shift**

After your practice, take 30 seconds to observe:

- How has your breathing changed?
- What's different in your body's sensations?
- How has your mental state evolved or settled?
- What business challenge might you approach differently now?

The power is in the conscious observation of the before-and-after states. This builds awareness of how quickly physical practices can influence your frequency.

## 🌿 CLOSING REFLECTION: RECLAIM YOUR BODY AS AN ENERGETIC ALLY

We've spent so long treating the body like a machine. Something to fix, sculpt, or control.

But your body is your portal to presence.

To intuition.
To power.
To pleasure.
To peace.

So move gently. Anchor deeply. Breathe bravely.

Let the earth hold you. Let your body guide you. Let your cells hum with coherence.

This is the path of embodied leadership. Not forcing your way through. But feeling your way forward.

One grounded step at a time.

# CHAPTER 16
# RHYTHMS OF REST AND REJUVENATION: RECLAIMING ENERGY THROUGH CYCLES, NOT HUSTLE

BY NOW, you've probably gathered that there was a time in my life when I never paused.

The pace was relentless. One task after the next. One problem to solve, one fire to put out. I didn't just resist rest—I felt guilty for needing it.

This guilt manifested as that voice whispering, "You haven't earned this break yet." It showed up as compulsively checking emails during family time and the nagging sensation that taking time for myself was somehow selfish.

However, I eventually learned that there is a difference between being tired and being disconnected.

When you are disconnected from your natural rhythms, your nervous system never truly resets. Your creativity flattens. Your clarity dulls. And your energy slowly depletes, day by day.

In earlier chapters, we explored how to regulate your state through the mind, body, and energy. Now, we turn to rhythm. The pause. The restoration.

Because sustainable success doesn't come from constantly doing, it comes from honoring the cycles of rest and rejuvenation—and giving yourself full permission to return to them.

## RECLAIMING THE SABBATH: THE SACRED PAUSE

In ancient cultures, the Sabbath was sacred. A time to step away from effort. To return to stillness. To reconnect with life—and self—on a deeper level.

You don't need to follow religious rules to reclaim this idea.

Today, the Sabbath becomes an energetic act of sovereignty.

A conscious withdrawal from hustle. A declaration that your value doesn't come from your productivity. A remembrance that space is where creativity is reborn.

My version of the Sabbath isn't complicated. It's slow mornings. No devices. Feet in the sand. Conversations that aren't about work. It's stillness. Breath. Space.

You don't need a whole day. Start with an hour. A morning. An afternoon.

I recall one Sunday when I was deeply involved in launching a new program. The pressure to keep working was intense. But I honored my commitment to a device-free morning. During my walk on the beach, completely unplugged, the solution to a marketing challenge I'd been struggling with for weeks suddenly appeared, fully formed.

This isn't coincidence. The breakthrough ideas, the fresh perspectives, the innovative solutions—they rarely come when we're pushing. They emerge in the spaces between effort.

## THE PERMISSION PARADOX: OVERCOMING REST GUILT

If you feel a twinge of discomfort or guilt even reading about taking time off, you're not alone. This resistance is deeply conditioned.

One woman I mentored would hide in the bathroom to read a novel for fifteen minutes, feeling she needed to conceal her "non-productive" time. When we worked together, she realized her most innovative business strategies emerged after these stolen moments of restoration.

The paradox is that giving yourself permission to rest doesn't diminish your productivity—it actually enhances it exponentially. However, you must first navigate the discomfort of challenging the "always-on" conditioning.

## PRACTICAL WAYS TO INTEGRATE REST

Not everyone can take an entire day off—and that's okay. What matters is your intention.

**For the extremely time-pressed:**

- **2-minute reset breaks:** Close your eyes and take five deep breaths between tasks
- **Mono-tasking:** Do just one thing with full presence, even if it's washing dishes
- **Screen-free transitions:** The ten minutes before bed and after waking

**When you have a bit more space:**

- **Set times for intentional rest:** Even 30-minute windows to read, nap, or breathe

- **Quality time with loved ones:** Emotional nourishment is energetic nourishment
- **Time in nature:** even short park walks can reset your frequency
- **Self-care rituals:** Baths, massages, or a candlelit meal just for you

These aren't indulgences. They're practices of presence. And presence raises your frequency.

Some of my greatest business breakthroughs have followed seasons of intentional rest. The six-figure program idea? It arrived during a meandering walk after three days of stepping back.

Rest isn't separate from productivity—it's its greatest ally.

## OPTIMIZING SLEEP: YOUR MOST POWERFUL RESET

Sleep isn't a luxury. It's a biological necessity. And one of the most effective tools for vibrational alignment.

When your sleep is disrupted, it doesn't just affect your mood. It affects:

- Your nervous system regulation
- Your hormone production
- Your emotional intelligence
- Your ability to create, respond, and lead
- Your intuitive capacity

For years, I hadn't connected the dots between my sleep patterns and my mood, focus, or ability to stay grounded in business. But once I began optimizing my sleep with simple, energetic practices, everything changed.

## CREATING A BEDROOM THAT SUPPORTS SLEEP

And it didn't just start with what I did *before* bed—it began with the space I slept in.

Your bedroom isn't just a room. It's an energetic sanctuary.

Every element within it communicates something to your nervous system. It either invites deep restoration or contributes to subtle stimulation and unrest.

Here are a few key adjustments I made that turned my sleep into a deeply restorative, high-frequency reset:

**1. Dimming Lights and Respecting Circadian Rhythms**

Our bodies are biologically wired to respond to natural light cycles. In the evening, the sun sets, light softens, and melatonin is released to help us fall asleep.

However, exposure to blue light, which is common in LED screens and bulbs, disrupts melatonin production. This tricks the brain into thinking it's still daylight and keeps your body in alert mode.

Practical upgrades:

- Avoid LED lighting once the sun sets. These energy-efficient bulbs emit higher levels of blue light and electromagnetic fields (EMFs).
- Use incandescent or halogen globes, which provide warmer, more sleep-friendly lighting.
- Use red-toned lighting, as red light has a minimal impact on melatonin levels and helps you wind down. Try red halogen lamps, Himalayan salt lamps, or even candlelight. This kind of lighting soothes the body and gently signals the brain that it's time to rest, without overstimulation.

**2. Protecting the Bedroom Frequency (EMFs)**

Many people unknowingly sleep in an environment that is highly stimulating to their energetic field.

This isn't just about noise or brightness—it's about EMFs.

Devices like routers, Bluetooth speakers, smart plugs, and even your phone emit low-level radiation that may impact:

- **Melatonin production:** Critical for sleep initiation
- **Brainwave activity:** Studies using EEGs have found that EMFs affect sleep-stage transitions
- **Sleep quality:** Including time spent in deep, restorative phases

Scientific research, as reported in The Journal of Pineal Research (2002), observed melatonin suppression due to EMF exposure, while Environmental Health Perspectives (2007) linked high EMFs to reduced sleep quality. Bioelectromagnetics (2012) reported EEG-detected changes in brain activity during sleep in the vicinity of EMFs.

While mainstream science hasn't reached a consensus on low-level EMFs, many experts advocate for a precautionary approach, especially during sleep.

Simple adjustments:

- Unplug WiFi routers at night or use a smart timer
- Turn off chargers and electronic devices near your bed
- Keep your phone in another room or on airplane mode

**3. EMF Shielding and Organite Tools**

If you live near high-EMF areas, such as busy urban centers or close to cell towers, consider experimenting with additional EMF protection.

Organite, a popular EMF-balancing device made of resin, metals, and quartz, is said to neutralize electromagnetic pollution by transmuting it into balanced energy.

While not scientifically verified in mainstream literature, many people report experiencing a calmer, more regulated, and energetic space after placing organite near their beds or electronic devices.

Energy is subtle, and you don't need absolute proof to honor what feels true in your body.

## WHEN REST FEELS IMPOSSIBLE

Even with the best intentions, establishing rest rhythms can be challenging.

For racing minds, use a worry journal to externalize thoughts before rest periods. For chaotic schedules, remember that micro-practices become even more important during intense periods.

The goal isn't perfect rest—it's progress toward a more sustainable rhythm.

---

## ◎ TRY THIS: DESIGN YOUR RHYTHM OF RESTORATION

Choose one way to honor your Sabbath this week:

- A device-free morning
- An afternoon in nature
- A no-work Sunday policy
- Saying "no" so you can stay home and rest

Then, choose one simple change to improve your sleep hygiene:

- Dim the lights after sunset
- Leave your phone outside your room, or turn it off
- Do a short meditation before bed
- Journal to release thoughts from your mind before sleep

<u>Remember</u>: it doesn't have to be perfect. Just intentional.

---

## CLOSING REFLECTION: REST AS FEMININE POWER

When you've been taught to overachieve, rest can feel uncomfortable. But the discomfort is not a sign that you're doing it wrong.

It's a sign that you're untangling from conditioning.

From "do more."
From "be useful."
From "keep going no matter what."

This conditioning runs deep in our cultural understanding of success, but it's particularly intense for women who have been taught that their value lies in service and constant output.

Authentic feminine leadership isn't about doing more—it's about tuning into your energy and responding accordingly.

Rested women are more magnetic. More intuitive. More impactful.

I've seen clients grow their businesses—not by working harder, but by learning to rest with strategy and intention. One built a six-figure coaching practice while maintaining firm boundaries around her work hours.

So, if your system has been whispering for pause—listen. Not because you're weak. But because you are finally strong enough to honor your natural rhythm.

Your body knows how to restore itself. You just need to get out of the way and let it.

## CHAPTER 17
# CONSCIOUS CONSUMPTION THAT SUPPORTS FREQUENCY, FOCUS, AND FLOW

JUST AS REST restores your energy, what you consume either amplifies or diminishes it.

After establishing rhythms of restoration, the next natural step is to examine what you're putting into your body. Together, these create the foundation for sustainable energy.

Your energy doesn't begin and end with your thoughts or sleep patterns. It's shaped by what you consume—what you eat, drink, apply, absorb, and expose yourself to daily.

This chapter isn't about perfection. It's about resonance.

It's not about rules. It's about conscious attunement.

Everything you consume carries a frequency. And that frequency either lifts you... or lowers you.

Once I started paying attention to how my food, water, environment, and habits were affecting me, my entire system recalibrated. The clearer my body became, the more clarity I had in business. The more I respected my vessel, the stronger my intuition became. And the more I consumed from with intention, not autopilot, the more radiant and energized I felt.

## THE STACKING APPROACH: ONE CHANGE AT A TIME

Before we delve into specifics, I would like to share my approach to these changes. I didn't overhaul everything overnight—that's a recipe for overwhelm and abandonment.

Instead, I found one change that felt manageable and resonant with me. I implemented it until it became routine. Then I added another. And another.

This "stacking" approach meant I never felt overwhelmed. Each change had time to integrate before I introduced something new.

I started with water quality because it felt accessible. Next, I upgraded my coffee routine. Months later, I explored deeper detox methods. Taking it step by step allowed these changes to become lasting habits rather than temporary "health kicks."

As you read through this chapter, don't pressure yourself to implement everything at once. Choose one element that calls to you. Master it. Then, build from there.

## FOOD AS FREQUENCY

Your body is electric. Your cells communicate through electrical signals and vibrations, so it makes sense that what you eat should support your energetic coherence.

Whole foods, especially those from the earth—fruits, vegetables, nuts, seeds, and herbs—are alive. They contain the sunlight, water, and minerals of their growth environment. This living energy transfers to you when consumed.

Processed foods, laden with additives, preservatives, and artificial chemicals? They're not just harder to digest. They lower your frequency and drain your energy reserves.

I'm not perfect with my diet, and I'm not suggesting you should be either. But when I started to become more intentional about how I fueled my body—more whole foods, less synthetic ones—I noticed real changes:

- More stable energy throughout the day (no more 3 p.m. crashes)
- Clearer thinking and faster decision-making
- Less bloating and brain fog
- A more vibrant emotional state
- Improved creativity and problem-solving

The results were most noticeable in my business. Client calls became more intuitive, content creation flowed more smoothly, and complex business decisions were made with greater clarity and confidence.

**Practical First Steps:**

- Start your day with a green smoothie (leafy greens + fruit + plant milk)
- Replace one processed snack with fresh fruit or vegetables
- Experiment with one plant-based dinner per week
- Read ingredients lists—if you can't pronounce it, consider alternatives

Tune into how food makes you feel, not just how it tastes. Let your energy be the feedback.

## WATER: THE LIVING MEMORY OF NATURE

Let's talk about water because not all water is created equal.

For years, I drank filtered water, assuming it was good enough. It's certainly better than tap water, which often contains chlorine, fluoride, and trace contaminants.

But what changed everything for me was learning about spring water—water that comes directly from the earth, still structured in its natural state.

Spring water holds the geometry of life. It's hexagonal in nature. It contains naturally occurring minerals. And, energetically, it's alive.

I first learned about this through the teachings of David Avocado Wolfe. I later explored the research of Masaru Emoto, whose work on water memory demonstrates how water is imprinted with the energy of its environment, including thoughts, music, and even intention.

When I switched to spring water, I noticed:

- Deeper hydration (I needed less water to feel satisfied)
- Clearer skin and eyes
- Improved digestion and detoxification
- Enhanced mental clarity during decision-making moments

**Practical Implementation:** If you can access fresh spring water, that's ideal. Use FindASpring.com to locate sources near you or search online for companies that might deliver it to you.

If not, consider investing in a high-quality filtration system that removes contaminants while preserving beneficial minerals. Simple options include:

- Berkey filters

- Reverse osmosis systems with remineralization
- Structured water devices

Store water in glass rather than plastic, which can leach chemicals and disrupt hormones.

Water is not just hydration. It's information. And your body, being 70–80% water, is always listening.

## COFFEE: CLEANING UP MY RITUAL

I've always loved coffee—the ritual, the warmth, the aroma.

But there came a time in my healing journey when I knew I needed to clean it up. I was relying on it too much. I'd wake up and reach for it before even checking in with how I felt.

So I started to:

- Switch to organic, mycotoxin-free beans (conventional coffee often contains mold toxins)
- Cut out processed dairy and sugar
- Blend it with coconut milk and a spoonful of raw honey
- Add raw cacao, which supports heart health, enhances mood with its natural PEA compounds, and contains vital minerals like magnesium
- Sometimes, add adaptogens like maca, medicinal mushrooms, or collagen

At first, the taste was different. But within a few weeks, regular café coffee tasted off to me. Now, that simple morning brew feels nourishing, not jittery.

It's a choice that supports my energy instead of taxing it.

For those wanting to reduce caffeine dependence:

- Start by delaying your first cup until after breakfast
- Experiment with half-caf blends
- Try dandelion coffee or mushroom elixirs as alternatives
- Consider matcha, which provides more stable energy

## ALCOHOL: ALIGNED USE, NOT AUTOMATIC USE

I went through a period of time where I would automatically reach for a glass of wine at the end of a hard day without thinking. It was just... normal.

But once I started paying attention to how it made me feel—physically, emotionally, energetically—I couldn't unsee it.

Poor sleep. Sluggish mornings. Lower vibration. And often, an emotional flatness the day after.

Alcohol is chemically disruptive, especially to your hormonal balance, nervous system, and sleep cycles.

This doesn't mean you have to cut it out completely. It just means you use it consciously.

In my case, I noticed alcohol's impact most directly on my mental clarity the following day. Important business decisions felt harder. Creative work required more effort. Client sessions lacked my usual intuitive flow.

When I became more intentional about alcohol:

- I saved it for true celebrations rather than stress relief
- I chose quality over quantity
- I stayed hydrated and supported my liver
- I tracked the results in my work and creativity

Ask yourself: *"Is this enhancing my clarity? Or muting it?"*

You might be surprised by the answer.

## DETOX PATHWAYS: CLEAR THE CHANNEL

You can't talk about vibrational health without addressing toxicity.

Your body has multiple detox systems working hard to remove what doesn't belong, not just physically but energetically. When those systems are overloaded, your energy slows down.

Let's look at the major ones.

**Liver**: Your liver processes everything—hormones, chemicals, medications, and even emotional stress. Support it with:

- Leafy greens and cruciferous vegetables
- Beetroot, lemon, dandelion tea, turmeric
- Reducing alcohol and synthetic additives

**Kidneys:** Responsible for fluid and mineral balance and deeply connected to adrenal health. Support them by:

- Drinking high-quality water (structured or filtered spring water)
- Reducing processed salt and excess caffeine
- Using gentle herbs like nettle, dandelion root, or parsley tea

**Lymphatic System:** Your lymph doesn't have a pump. It needs movement. Support it with:

- Rebounding (mini trampoline) – even 5 minutes daily helps
- Dry brushing before showering
- Infrared saunas or hot-cold therapy
- Walking and stretching

**Skin:** Your largest organ—and a key detox channel. Support it by:

- Sweating (saunas, movement)
- Using natural skincare products
- Drinking clean water and eating antioxidants

**Lungs:** Your breath is a detox tool. Support it with:

- Breathwork and pranayama
- Opening your windows to bring in fresh air
- Reducing synthetic fragrance and aerosols

**Colon:** This is where things get... real.

If your colon isn't eliminating efficiently, waste and toxicity can recirculate in the body.

For years, I resisted practices like colonics or coffee enemas. I found the idea of them invasive and awkward.

But when my health became a priority, I decided to try.

And you know what? It wasn't as bad as I imagined. In fact, I felt lighter, more energized, and clearer afterwards—not just physically, but emotionally too.

The benefits far outweighed my initial resistance.

These practices aren't for everyone, and they should always be done safely and with support. But for me, they became part of my deeper release, clearing not just waste, but old emotional density held in the gut.

## WHEN IT FEELS OVERWHELMING: PERMISSION TO BEGIN SMALL

I want to acknowledge something important: health information can be overwhelming.

There are endless opinions, conflicting research, and so many "shoulds."

This is why I advocate for the stacking approach. Don't try to implement everything at once. Start with what resonates most.

Maybe it's upgrading your water.

Maybe it's adding a green smoothie.

Maybe it's dry brushing before your shower.

Choose one practice. Give yourself 14-21 days to integrate it. Then add another if it feels right.

There's no rush. This isn't a race to perfection.

It's a gradual elevation in how you treat your body, which directly impacts how clearly you think, how confidently you make decisions, and how confidently and authentically you show up in your business and life.

---

## ◎ TRY THIS: CONSCIOUS RESET REFLECTION

- What foods or drinks are you consuming that no longer feel aligned?
- What's one small detox ritual you could try this week? (e.g., dry brushing, herbal tea, swapping dairy milk for coconut milk)
- Where are you consuming from autopilot, and how bring more intention to those choices?

## 🦋 CLOSING REFLECTION: YOU'RE NOT BEING RIGID—YOU'RE BEING REVERENT

This isn't about discipline. It's about devotion.

Devotion to your body. To your energy. To your future self.

You don't need to overhaul everything overnight. Just tune in. Listen. And begin to choose what expands you—from the inside out.

Because when you consume with consciousness, you don't just change what's on your plate.

You change what becomes possible in your life and business.

# CHAPTER 18
# CREATING FLOW IN WORK AND LIFE

THERE'S a reason why some days feel effortless—and others feel like you're dragging yourself through molasses.

It's not always about discipline. It's about flow.

And flow doesn't happen by accident. It's something we create intentionally—by setting up our internal and external environments to support it.

When we remove resistance, align with rhythm, and design environments that support our energetic state, flow becomes our default, not the exception.

## WHAT IS FLOW, REALLY?

Flow is a term coined by psychologist Mihaly Csikszentmihalyi, describing a mental state in which we're fully immersed in what we're doing—completely engaged, energized, and often unaware of time (Csikszentmihalyi, 1990).

You've felt it before.

When the words poured effortlessly onto the page.
When hours disappeared in the studio.
When a coaching session felt like channelled wisdom.
When your body moved and your mind disappeared.

Flow is when your inner and outer worlds sync. It's where joy meets productivity—and burnout disappears.

For women entrepreneurs, finding flow isn't just about productivity—it's about sustainability. It's how we build businesses that energize rather than deplete us.

## PREPARING FOR FLOW—BEFORE YOU EVEN SIT DOWN

Flow doesn't begin the moment your fingers hit the keyboard.

It begins long before that—in the way you start your day.

If you've been following the practices in earlier chapters—rising gently, grounding yourself, nourishing your body, connecting to intention—then you've already been cultivating a high-vibrational state from the moment you woke up.

That's not just a feel-good ritual.

That's the setup for flow.

The last thing you want is to arrive in your workspace—full of presence, aligned in your energy—and be met with visual clutter, mental chaos, and a desk that lowers your frequency.

Flow can't thrive in an environment disrupts your focus and clarity.

That's why creating physical and energetic clarity in your workspace matters. It preserves and amplifies the state you've cultivated.

When your rituals, body, and environment are working together, flow becomes the natural next step.

You're not forcing focus. You're riding a frequency.

## DESIGNING A SPACE THAT SUPPORTS YOU

Your space holds a frequency.

When your workspace is cluttered, stagnant, or overstimulating, it creates subtle resistance that your nervous system detects—even if you're not consciously aware of it.

Simple upgrades that make a massive difference:

- **Natural light:** boosts dopamine and supports circadian rhythms
- **Nature views:** even a plant or a desktop background of the ocean calms the nervous system
- **Visual harmony:** less clutter = more clarity
- **Soundscapes:** instrumental music, binaural beats, café ambience, or ocean waves—whatever helps you tune in

One of my favourites? The gentle sounds of the ocean surf while I write. It's grounding, rhythmic, and spacious.

Don't wait for the perfect Pinterest office. Create flow with what you've got.

## SACRED SCHEDULING: BUILDING RHYTHMS THAT WORK

Structure used to feel restrictive to me—something that would stifle my creativity. But once I realized that rhythm is different from rigidity, everything changed.

The feminine thrives in cycles, not chaos.

Now, I work with my energy, not against it.

Some of my practices include:

- **Time blocking with spaciousness**: Protected creation windows that aren't crammed edge-to-edge
- **Themed days**: Client calls on Tuesday and Wednesday, content creation on Thursday, strategy and planning on Friday
- **White space**: Time that isn't assigned, so I can recalibrate if needed
- **Cyclical planning**: Adjusting my workload to honor my hormonal, emotional, or seasonal energy

I also honour when I need to stop—even mid-task—if I feel I've lost presence. Sometimes, 10 minutes of walking barefoot in the garden can reset my whole nervous system and bring me back to clarity.

Your energy is your most valuable resource. Protect it with rhythms that support your flow, not just your to-do list.

## FLOW IN TRANSITION MOMENTS

As women entrepreneurs, many of us navigate multiple roles throughout our day. We move from CEO to content creator to mom to partner—sometimes within the span of just a few hours.

These transitions can either drain us or become intentional reset points.

One client, Sarah, a branding strategist and mother of two, created a 3-minute ritual between client calls and school pickups: three deep breaths, a face mist with essential oils, and setting a clear intention for the next phase of her day. This simple practice helped her maintain presence across roles rather than carry the energy of one space into another.

Try creating mini-rituals for your transitions:

- A specific song between tasks

- A short visualization before meeting with clients
- A physical gesture (like standing and stretching) when transitioning between roles

These small moments of intentional transition preserve your energy and allow you to show up fully in each space.

## DIGITAL FLOW: THE UNSEEN DISRUPTOR

You could have a beautiful space and a perfect schedule, but if your phone is pinging every 12 seconds, you'll struggle to stay in the flow.

Digital chaos fragments your focus and lowers your vibrational state.

A few boundaries that support me:

- All non-essential notifications OFF
- All tabs closed before finishing the day—yes, all of them
- Social media batch times—no more passive scrolling between tasks
- "Do Not Disturb" mode during creative sprints
- Only checking emails at designated times

This isn't about control. It's about preserving your peace.

For those of you who manage teams, consider implementing "flow hours"—dedicated time blocks where your team knows not to expect immediate responses, allowing everyone deeper focus time.

---

## ◎ TRY THIS: YOUR FLOW ACTIVATION RITUAL

Today or this week, try the following:

**Reset one environment:** Your desk, inbox, or even your kitchen bench. Let it reflect your energy, not your past chaos.

**Choose one pre-flow ritual**: A five-minute breath practice, a favorite playlist, or a mantra that anchors you into presence.

**Audit your schedule:**

- Where are you leaking energy?
- Where do you feel supported?
- What could be realigned to support your most focused, creative self?

---

## CLOSING REFLECTION: FLOW IS AN ACT OF FEMININE LEADERSHIP

You're not here to grind your way to success. You're here to flow into it. To design your space and time in a way that honors your brilliance, not burns it out. Flow doesn't arrive when everything is perfect. Flow arrives when you become intentional.

About your energy.

About your space.

About your rhythm.

So the next time you find yourself stuck, scattered, or uninspired—don't force.

Clear the noise. Come back to stillness. And choose to build your flow, moment by moment.

Because when your work is an extension of your soul, flow becomes your default setting.

# INTEGRATION POINT: TRANSITIONING FROM SHIFT TO RISE

As we conclude Part II: *The Shift*, let's take a moment to reflect on the journey so far.

In Part I: *The Root*, we examined the foundations of your being—understanding your current reality and the patterns that have shaped your life and business. We explored how to recognize limiting beliefs and create space for new possibilities.

In Part II: *The Shift*, we've covered practical tools to interrupt those old patterns and create new ones aligned with your soul's calling. From grounding morning rituals to releasing what no longer serves you, from honoring your body's natural rhythms to creating environments that support your highest vibration, these practices have balanced masculine structure with feminine flow.

Now, you stand at the threshold of Part III: *The Rise*.

This is where everything comes together—where embodiment meets expression, where your internal work manifests in external leadership. The practices you've been cultivating aren't just personal development tools; they're the building blocks of a new way of showing up in the world.

In the coming chapters, you'll discover how to embrace the journey of growth, even when it's uncomfortable. You'll learn to recognize how your external reality mirrors your internal state and how to pivot with grace when life calls for adaptation. We'll explore building aligned communities, leading from the heart, and making decisions from your highest frequency.

This final section invites you to step fully into your authentic expression, create a meaningful legacy, and align with your soul's purpose. It's the moment your story expands from internal to shared—where your journey inspires others to rise.

*The Rise* isn't about reaching a destination. It's about embodying the journey itself.

It's time to rise.

The world is waiting for exactly who you're becoming.

# PART THREE
# THE RISE

## CHAPTER 19
# BECOMING THE WOMAN WHO RISES: EMBRACING GROWTH AS A WAY OF BEING

THROUGHOUT PART II, we've explored the practical rituals and habits that build a foundation for your energetic well-being—from morning practices and meditation to mindful consumption and creating environments that support your flow. These are the daily choices that gradually elevate your frequency and capacity.

But what happens when, despite your best practices, life throws you a curveball that no morning ritual seems capable of catching? What about those moments when your carefully crafted systems suddenly feel inadequate in the face of a real challenge?

This is where we need to delve deeper because growth isn't neat.

It's not linear.
It's not always pretty.
And it certainly isn't predictable.

Despite what we might like to believe, building a life or business that's aligned with your soul doesn't follow a perfect upward trajectory.

It spirals. It loops. It pulls you back just when you think you're moving forward. It stretches you in places you thought you'd already healed.

And more often than not... It's uncomfortable.

## THE DARKEST CHAPTER OF MY LIFE

If I think back to the most uncomfortable—no, *excruciating*—season of my life, it was when I plunged into a deep depression and chronic anxiety.

At the time, it didn't feel like a "growth moment." It felt like drowning.

I remember honestly believing that this was going to be my new reality. That the anxiety would never leave. That the heaviness would never lift. That the spark I once had was gone—and might never return.

But here's the miracle...

That experience, as agonising as it was, became the very thing that brought me to this work. It cracked me open.

It led me to discover what I'm now teaching you—about vibrational health, energetic awareness, trauma, healing, and integration.

It put me on the path of *becoming*.

And if I could go back and erase it?

I wouldn't.
Because that pit... **was the *gift*.**

Your entrepreneurial journey might not mirror my experience with depression, but I've noticed that even when my clients are diligent with their morning rituals, mindful with their consumption habits, and disciplined with their environments—as we explored in Part II—they still encounter valleys that test their resolve. Those moments when a launch fails, when clients leave, when the algorithm changes overnight require something beyond routine. They demand a different relationship with discomfort itself.

## DISCOMFORT IS NOT A SIGN YOU'RE FAILING

In business, discomfort shows up in a thousand different ways.

The launch that flops. The customer complaint that shakes your confidence. The team challenge that pushes every button you've got. The financial cliff edge that wakes you at 2 a.m. with a tight chest and spiralling thoughts.

But here's what I want you to remember:

Discomfort isn't a red flag. It's an invitation.
It's showing you the edges of your current energetic container.
And it's asking: *Are you willing to expand?*

This understanding transformed not just my personal healing but also how I approach every aspect of business and life. The daily practices we've been cultivating—the meditation, the breathwork, the conscious consumption—don't exist to help us avoid discomfort. They exist to enhance our capacity to navigate it with presence.

So when my first digital course launch failed to meet even half of my financial goals, no amount of morning journaling could shield me from that sting of disappointment. But the presence I'd developed through those practices gave me something far more valuable than protection: it gave me *perspective*.

And with that perspective came a choice—one we all face in moments of emotional contraction: Would I retreat into shame and self-doubt, or lean in with curiosity and courage to meet what this moment was here to teach me?

## LEANING IN: GROWTH REQUIRES PRESENCE

Most of us are taught to retreat from discomfort. To distract, deny, or suppress.

But true growth happens when we lean in.

Not to suffer unnecessarily—but to feel fully. To allow what's here to be seen, acknowledged, and alchemised.

As we explored earlier through Singer's work, this is the essence of radical acceptance—the practice of meeting life exactly as it is, without resistance..

It doesn't mean you like what's happening. It means you stop fighting the reality long enough to extract its wisdom.

Buddhist teacher and author Pema Chödrön emphasizes this approach, teaching that the only way to ease our pain is to experience it fully. She encourages us to "learn to stay with uneasiness, learn to stay with the tightening," so that our habitual reactions don't continue to rule our lives.

By meeting discomfort with presence and compassion, we open the door to growth and freedom.

As Brené Brown teaches, embracing our vulnerability—acknowledging that we don't have it all together—is a pathway to genuine strength.

I've watched this pattern repeat for countless entrepreneurs in my community. The physical practices, the mindful consumption, the environment optimization we explored in Part II—they create the container. But it's how we respond when that container is tested that determines our growth.

## THE PIT BECOMES THE PORTAL

There are moments that feel like collapse. Like failure. Like it's all coming undone.

But often, those moments are precisely what are needed to unravel so something truer can emerge.

The failed partnership that forces you to clarify your true vision. The cancelled program that reveals what your audience actually needs. The business model that collapses so that a more sustainable one can emerge.

Hawkins taught that even our lowest emotional states—such as grief, fear, and guilt—hold within them the seeds of evolution. If we meet them with consciousness, they become gateways to a deeper understanding.

The pit becomes the portal. The wound becomes the womb of something new. The breakdown becomes the breakthrough.

I've lived that truth. And I know many of you have, too—or will.

---

## 🌀 TRY THIS: REFRAMING RESISTANCE

Take a moment to check in.

*Where am I feeling discomfort right now—in business, in life, in my body?*
*What might this moment be asking me to feel, to face, or to release?*
*What part of me is being invited to expand?*

Don't try to solve it all today. Just notice.

Discomfort isn't a detour. It's the doorway.

This is why all the habits and practices we've been building aren't just about feeling good or optimizing performance, though they certainly help with both. They're about developing the inner strength to meet life's challenges with an open heart and a clear mind.

The grounding practices, the cold therapy, the conscious media consumption—they're training for these moments that matter most. They're preparing you to recognize discomfort not as a signal to retreat but as an invitation to expand.

---

## CLOSING REFLECTION: THIS IS THE WORK

Real growth is messy. It's rarely polished. And it never happens in a straight line.

But it always moves you forward—even when it feels like you've been brought to your knees.

You're not behind. You're not broken. You're not failing.

You're growing.

And this discomfort you're feeling? It's the stretch of becoming.

So, take a breath.
Soften the resistance.
And lean in.

Because the next version of you—the woman you're here to become—is waiting on the other side.

# CHAPTER 20
# THE ART OF PIVOTING: NAVIGATING CHANGE WITH GRACE, PURPOSE, AND POWER

"I'M SORRY, Ms. Soutter, but there's been another production delay. We can't guarantee shipping until December 15th."

My stomach dropped.

The new range—my biggest product development of the year—wouldn't arrive until after Christmas. After months of designing, sampling, photographing, and pre-marketing, the cornerstone of my Q4 revenue projections had just collapsed.

My first reaction?

Tightness in my chest.
The urge to force a solution.
To pressure the manufacturer, expedite shipping at exorbitant costs, or launch anyway and risk disappointing customers.

But then I remembered: this feeling was familiar. It was the **energy of resistance.**

There will be times when things just don't go to plan.

You're doing the work. You're aligned with your values. You're following the energy. And still, the deal falls through. The team member quits. The product flops.

It can feel frustrating—even defeating, especially if you've poured your heart into something.

But here's what's real: part of living and leading from a place of energetic integrity is learning how to pivot.

Not from panic.
Not from fear.
But from presence, acceptance, and wisdom.

In earlier chapters, we explored the power of surrender (Chapter 5) and the distinction between power and force (Chapter 8). That foundation becomes essential here. Because pivoting isn't about abandoning your goals, it's about releasing the grip on how you thought things *had* to unfold.

## THE ENERGY OF RESISTANCE VS. FLOW

When something isn't working, our instinct is often to double down. Push harder. Force it into shape.

But if the energy feels off—if there's resistance, friction, breakdowns—then forcing is only going to magnify the problem.

This is where you step into vibrational awareness:

> *Is my current strategy aligned, or am I forcing something that no longer serves me?*

In her book, *Be Water, My Friend*, Shannon Lee shares the moment she realized she had to let go of a project she loved:

"I gave the future of the project to the universe, and I said, 'Show me the way.' And like water, I began to follow the course of this new unfolding rather than try to build a thousand dams to enforce the direction of the stream."

This is the art of the pivot.

Not giving up. Not failing.

Pivoting is participation without control. Presence without panic. Fluidity without flakiness.

> "I'm participating and co-creating, but no longer forcing."
>
> SHANNON LEE

## WHEN THE PATH CHANGES

Sometimes, things fall apart not because you're off track but because something greater is trying to emerge.

I've had launches fail that later revealed gaps I hadn't noticed—like the online course that flopped but showed me my audience wanted high-touch consulting instead.

I've had team changes that felt like setbacks but ended up bringing in the *right* people—like when my social media manager quit unexpectedly, only for me to find someone with expertise in both content *and* e-commerce.

I've had moments when I resisted letting go—such as holding onto a low-performing product line because I loved the concept—only to find deep peace and better profits when I finally did.

**Pivoting isn't a detour. It's a recalibration.**

It's your higher self saying: *There's another way.*

## THE POWER OF PRESENCE

As we've discussed throughout this book, presence is your superpower. When you stay present with what *is, rather than clinging to what was meant to be, you open yourself* to real-time guidance. You become like water:

- Flowing around obstacles
- Adapting without losing your essence
- Reclaiming your power through surrender

Presence lets you see the opportunity in the breakdown. The wisdom in the delay. The redirection in the rejection.

And yes, it's not always immediate. Sometimes, you have to grieve what didn't go the way you planned. But in that softening, something else arises:

Creativity. Clarity. Courage.

---

## 🌀 TRY THIS: THE PIVOT PAUSE

When you feel resistance building, take what I call a **Pivot Pause**:

1. **Breathe & Center**: Take three deep breaths into your heart space
2. **Notice**: Where in your body do you feel the resistance?
3. **Ask**: What am I trying to force right now?
4. **Release**: Imagine letting go of your grip on the outcome
5. **Open**: What new possibility might be trying to emerge?

This 2-minute reset can move your entire energy from force to flow.

## PIVOTING IN BUSINESS: A PRACTICAL VIEW

Let's talk real world for a moment.

In entrepreneurship, pivoting might look like this:

**Product Pivots:**

- When my "Mentoring Mums Online" program wasn't selling, I took the same program, rebranded it for small business owners, and tripled my conversion rate
- Pivoting from physical products to digital when supply chain issues hit
- Changing your packaging after customer feedback on sustainability

**Marketing Pivots:**

- Reallocating ad spend from Facebook to TikTok when algorithms change
- Moving from long-form content to short-form video based on engagement metrics
- Updating your messaging when market research reveals new customer pain points

**Business Model Pivots:**

- Transitioning from one-time sales to subscription revenue
- Repositioning your offer from B2C to B2B when you discover higher value opportunities
- Moving from service provider to product creator (or vice versa)

**Personal Brand Pivots:**

- Refining your niche after discovering where your true zone of genius lies
- Changing your positioning when your personal values evolve
- Embracing a new platform or medium that better showcases your strengths

The difference is *how* you pivot.

From fear? You'll shrink, scramble, and sabotage.
From power? You'll adapt, align, and rise.

When you've done the inner work—like the Energy Audit (Chapter 6) and Reframing Your Language (Chapter 9)—pivoting becomes a skill, not a panic button.

You *notice* when things aren't flowing. You *listen* for guidance. You *move* in the direction of coherence.

## CASE STUDY: MY BOOK LAUNCH PIVOT

When I released my first book, I had a clear vision: a traditional publishing route, a major publicity campaign, and a national book tour.

But as I shared in Chapter 12, the energy felt heavy. Each pitch and proposal required enormous effort, and the rejections piled up.

Instead of forcing, I paused. I checked in with my energy.

The question wasn't *"How do I make this work?"*
It was *"What wants to emerge here?"*

What emerged was a completely different path: self-publishing with a direct-to-reader approach. Building my own platform. Creating intimate virtual events instead of exhausting tours.

The result? Not only more sales than I projected, but deeper reader connections, achieved complete creative control, and a business model that felt energetically aligned.

Was it the path I expected? No.
Was it the right path? **Absolutely**.

---

## 🌀 TRY THIS: ENERGY CHECKPOINT FOR DECISION-MAKING

Next time you're faced with a crossroads, ask:

- Am I forcing or flowing?
- What am I afraid will happen if I change course?
- Where does my energy feel light when I consider the options?
- What is the next aligned action that feels true?

Let those answers guide your next move.

---

## CLOSING REFLECTION: BE WATER, NOT THE DAM

There is a quiet power in knowing when to pivot.

It says: *I trust myself.*
It says: *I'm not attached to the outcome—I'm loyal to my inner knowing.*

It says: *I am fluid, resilient, and creative.*

Being like water doesn't mean being passive. It means choosing grace over resistance. It means responding, not reacting. It means moving forward with trust in what's unfolding.

And when you pivot—not from fear, but from presence—you're no longer forcing outcomes. You're accessing a deeper strength.

As Hawkins teaches in *Power vs. Force*, real power arises from higher states of consciousness, such as love, acceptance, and peace. Force, by contrast, stems from control, fear, and resistance. One drains your energy. The other expands it.

So when the partnership falls through, the launch underperforms, or the strategy hits a wall, remember:

You're not starting over. You're being redirected.
You're not failing. You're evolving.
You're not losing your way. You're finding a better one.

Let this be your mantra in moments of transition:

> *I am participating and co-creating. But I am no longer forcing.*

This is the art of the pivot.
This is how you rise.

## CHAPTER 21
# FINDING YOUR PEOPLE: BUILDING A COMMUNITY THAT NOURISHES AND ELEVATES YOU

WHEN I FIRST LEFT THE world of being an employee and stepped into entrepreneurship, it was electrifying.

I had freedom. Creative control. Autonomy.

I could work when I wanted, where I wanted, and how I wanted.

The possibilities felt endless.

But as the initial thrill began to settle, I started to feel something else:

Loneliness.

There were days when I felt completely alone, especially when challenges arose and I had no one to bounce ideas off. No team to turn to. No co-worker to offer a second opinion over coffee.

Some days, I wondered if I'd made a mistake.

Would it be easier to go back to working for someone else? Back to structure? Back to certainty?

What I missed most in those moments wasn't the security. It was the connection.

The kind of connection that comes from being around people who truly *get* you. People who see your vision. Support your growth. Challenge you when you shrink.

Over time, I started to find those people.

I found entrepreneurial communities where I could share openly. Spaces where others were walking a similar path. Mentors who could hold up the mirror and help me rise.

And that changed everything.

The right community became a lifeline. Not just for my business—but for my energy, my confidence, and my clarity.

That's what this chapter is about: Building the support network that lifts you, stretches you, and reminds you that you are not meant to do this alone.

## THE PEOPLE YOU SURROUND YOURSELF WITH MATTER

Jim Rohn famously said, *"You are the average of the five people you spend the most time with."*

When you think about the people you regularly engage with, are they expanding you? Or contracting you?

In business—especially as a soul-driven entrepreneur—you'll face doubt, big decisions, and moments where it's easy to forget who you are.

The right community is a mirror. It reflects your power when you forget. It believes in your mission when you wobble. It helps you hold the vision when the fear creeps in.

The right community offers:

- **Energetic support**: People who *see* you and remind you of your truth
- **Shared momentum**: Spaces where everyone is rising together
- **Accountability**: Loving mirrors that hold you to your highest standard
- **Expansion**: Conversations that stretch your mind and grow your heart

Your environment matters. And that includes your people.

## THE HIDDEN ROI OF COMMUNITY

When we think of business investments, we often focus on tangible assets: Software. Advertising. Inventory. Website development.

But I've witnessed time and again that the highest return on investment comes from something less tangible: The right community.

One of my e-commerce clients, Sarah, was ready to close her online store after months of disappointing sales. She had the right products, beautiful branding, and solid marketing—but something wasn't clicking.

During one of our fortnightly strategy calls, she confessed, "I feel like I'm shouting into the void. Like no one cares if I succeed or fail."

After checking in on her mindset and energy levels, I recommended specific tools from our work together to help her realign her energy. We also focused on connecting her with a community of shop owners in her particular niche. Within three months, those relationships had yielded:

- Cross-promotion opportunities that doubled her email list
- A product collaboration that became her bestseller
- Access to niche-specific expertise she couldn't find elsewhere
- Emotional support from people who understood her exact market challenges

Most importantly? She didn't quit.

"I would have given up months ago without this circle," she told me. "Having people who understood exactly what I was going through made all the difference."

And she's not alone. Again and again, I've witnessed how community changes the game—not just for strategy or visibility, but for staying the course when the path gets tough.

The ROI isn't just emotional, though that matters tremendously. It's also:

- **Financial:** Communities generate referrals, collaborations, and shared resources
- **Strategic:** Different perspectives help you see blind spots and opportunities
- **Exponential:** Your network's network becomes your extended resource
- **Sustainable:** Community support prevents burnout and promotes longevity

As entrepreneurs, we're taught to value independence. But the most successful business owners I know understand interdependence.

So how do you find or build a community that offers that kind of return?

Here are three models that work:

**1. The Structured Mastermind**

A small group (4-8 people) that meets regularly with a clear structure and accountability.

**What makes it work:**

- Consistent meeting cadence (weekly/bi-weekly/monthly)
- Similar business stage but diverse perspectives
- Structured sharing format (wins, challenges, requests)
- Clear commitments between meetings

**Real-world example:** My mastermind meets for 90 minutes every two weeks. We begin with celebrations, move to current challenges, and end with specific commitments. The format ensures everyone gets equal airtime and leaves with actionable next steps.

**2. The Digital Sanctuary**

An online space where entrepreneurs connect daily without geographical limitations.

**What makes it work:**

- Clear community values and guidelines
- Regular engagement prompts and check-ins
- Multiple connection formats (text, voice, video)
- Boundaries around promotion vs. contribution

**Real-world example:** Facebook groups and private communities can offer genuine connection and be places to find your people, but not all groups are created equal. Be discerning about which ones you join.

Free groups often attract beginners who are still finding their way, which is ideal if you're just starting out. The questions are simpler. The energy is exploratory. As you advance in your journey, you might need something different. Paid communities typically attract more seasoned entrepreneurs who understand your advanced challenges and speak your language.

Select spaces that reflect your current level of expertise. Where the conversations feed rather than drain you. Where the energy feels aligned with yours.

**3. The Mentor Relationship**

One-to-one guidance from someone who's walked the path before you.

**What makes it work:**

- Regular check-ins with honest feedback
- Someone who sees your blind spots and potential
- Accountability with compassion
- A safe space for vulnerability

**Real-world example:** In my mentoring work, I support entrepreneurs with both strategic guidance and the inner shifts required to move beyond self-sabotage, limiting beliefs, and emotional blocks. Yes, we cover business models, marketing tactics, and scaling strategies—but the foundation is far more holistic. My approach integrates all the concepts we've explored in this book: energy awareness, emotional intelligence, subconscious programming, language patterns, vibrational alignment, and authentic leadership.

Clients receive direct WhatsApp access for real-time support, alongside regular strategy calls where we align their vision with practical execution. However, during these sessions, I also tune into their energy, listen for language that reveals self-sabotage or limiting beliefs, and gently guide them back into coherence.

Because true growth isn't just about external action—it's about the frequency with which that action is taken. This is what makes the mentoring so impactful. It's business mentoring, yes—but grounded in the full spectrum of what it means to rise.

## NURTURING HIGH-FREQUENCY RELATIONSHIPS

As your vibration rises, not all relationships will come with you.

Some will naturally fall away. And that's okay. It doesn't mean you've outgrown them. It just means your energy is evolving.

Honour them with love. Release with grace. And then, go find your people. The ones who resonate. The ones who *remember* who you are.

Just like we explored in *The Mirror Principle*, your external world reflects your internal energy.

Want to attract high-vibe, soul-aligned connections? Start by becoming that energy yourself.

Operate with integrity. Speak your truth. Take aligned action.

As you rise, so will your circle.

Here's how to start:

**1. Get Clear on What You Crave**

What kind of people do you want around you?
What qualities do they have?
Are they grounded?
Growth-oriented?
Kind?
Candid?

Make a list. Tune into how it *feels* to be around those kinds of people.

**2. Step Into the Spaces Where They Gather**

That might be:

- Masterminds
- Women's circles
- Online memberships
- Retreats
- Community events
- Spiritual workshops

The key? Go where growth is the norm. Go where energy feels clean.

**3. Deepen. Don't Just Network.**

You're not here for surface-level small talk. You're here for depth. For soul. For *realness*.

So share openly. Ask meaningful questions. Follow up. Be the kind of connection you wish to find.

**4. Be Willing to Be Seen**

You don't attract soul-aligned people by wearing a mask. You attract them by being real. Messy. Honest. Human.

It might feel scary at first. But it's how true belonging begins.

**5. Give Before You Get**

Support others. Share their work. Celebrate their wins. Offer introductions. Add value.

Connection thrives in generosity. What you give will return tenfold, just not always from where you expect.

**6. Protect Your Field**

Not everyone deserves access to you. That's not cold. It's wise.

Boundaries create space for your best connections to flourish. Choose your front row wisely.

## OVERCOMING COMMUNITY BARRIERS

Despite recognizing the importance of community, many entrepreneurs struggle to find their ideal community or tribe. Here's why—and how to move past these common blocks:

**The Scarcity Mindset**

*"There's not enough success to go around."*

When we operate from a scarcity mindset, we view other entrepreneurs as competitors rather than potential collaborators. We hold back, protect our ideas, and miss opportunities to connect.

**The Shift:** Remember that abundance is your natural state. There are more than enough clients, opportunities, and resources for everyone. The entrepreneur who shares freely often receives most abundantly.

**The Perfectionism Trap**

*"I'll reach out when my business is more successful."*

Many wait until they feel "successful enough" to join certain communities or approach potential collaborators. But the right community meets you where you are and helps you grow.

**The Shift:** Your journey—including the messy parts—is your greatest connector. Share authentically from where you stand today. The right people will resonate with your realness, not just your results.

**The Independence Illusion**

*"Needing others means I'm not strong enough."*

Our culture often glorifies the "self-made" entrepreneur. We internalize the belief that asking for help or connection signals weakness.

**The Shift:** True strength lies in knowing when to reach out. The most successful entrepreneurs I've mentored actively seek support, feedback, and connection. They understand that interdependence—not independence—is the goal.

## A PERSONAL NOTE ON MENTORSHIP

In my role as a mentor, I've witnessed something remarkable time and again: the power of not being alone.

I regularly receive messages from clients saying things like:

*"I would have given up months ago if not for your encouragement."*

*"I've made more progress in three months with you than in three years on my own."*

*"For the first time, I feel like someone actually gets my vision."*

These messages aren't about my advice or strategies, though those matter. They're about being seen. Being held. Having someone who believes in your vision when doubt creeps in.

That's the power of the right mentor and the right community.

When you're considering giving up... When your launch doesn't perform as expected... When you face a challenge that feels insurmountable...

Having someone who's walked the path before you—who can shine a light on the way forward—makes all the difference.

Your tribe doesn't just support your business. They hold your heart. They remind you of your power. They call you forward.

And you do the same in return.

## 🌀 TRY THIS: COMMUNITY CLARITY EXERCISE

1. List five traits you want in your aligned tribe.
2. Reflect: Are you embodying those traits yourself?
3. Identify three places (online or offline) where they might gather.
4. Take one aligned action to connect with someone new this week.
5. Write down three ways you could contribute value to a community before asking for anything in return.

## CLOSING REFLECTION: YOU'RE NOT MEANT TO RISE ALONE

It's easy to romanticize the lone wolf. To believe that strength means doing it all yourself. But true strength is knowing when to reach out. When to be held. When to walk beside others who remind you of your light.

You don't need a massive following. You don't need a huge network.

You just need real, aligned connection. A few people who see you. Who get it. Who mirror your growth, your joy, and your power.

When entrepreneurs find their people, everything begins to open up—their business expands, and their life becomes more aligned. I've watched women who were ready to give up go on to build thriving companies because someone believed in them. I've witnessed the power of a well-timed voice note saying, *"I see you, and you can do this."*

Your people exist. And they're looking for you, too.

Let who you are—fully, authentically, and unapologetically—be the signal that calls them in.

And remember: as you rise, reach back. Be the mirror for someone else. Hold the space that was once held for you.

This is how we all rise together.

# CHAPTER 22
# LEADING FROM LOVE, NOT FEAR IN BUSINESS AND LIFE

I STOOD at the crossroads of a major business decision.

A competitor had just launched a nearly identical product to my bestseller—at half the price.

My team was panicking. My advisors urged immediate action:

*"Cut your prices."*
*"Run aggressive counter-marketing."*
*"Fight back before they steal your market share."*

My stomach tightened. My thoughts raced. Everything in me wanted to react—to protect what I'd built.

But in that moment of contraction, I recognized something: I was making decisions from fear.

I paused. Took a breath. And asked myself a simple question: **How would love respond?**

Not soft, fuzzy love. Strategic love. Love that sees beyond the immediate threat to the bigger picture.

Instead of slashing prices, we doubled down on customer experience. Instead of attacking our competitor, we elevated our messaging. Instead of fighting for market share, we focused on deepening loyalty.

Within three months, an interesting thing happened. Our sales actually increased. Our customer retention strengthened. Our competitor's "race to the bottom" pricing became unsustainable.

This wasn't just a lucky break. It was the tangible difference between acting from fear versus acting from love.

## THE VIBRATIONAL IMPACT OF FEAR VS. LOVE

Every decision we make carries an energetic signature.

As we explored in Chapter 8 using Hawkins' Scale of Consciousness, different emotional states vibrate at varying frequencies, profoundly affecting our ability to make wise decisions.

As we've seen, fear operates at a lower frequency. It contracts our awareness, narrows our options, and triggers our survival response.

Love, by contrast, vibrates at a significantly higher frequency. It expands our awareness, opens us to possibilities, and activates our creative centers.

When we operate from fear, we access only a fraction of our intelligence. When we operate from love, we tap into our full capacity.

This isn't just spiritual theory. It's backed by neuroscience.

Research from the HeartMath Institute reveals that the heart possesses its own complex nervous system, referred to by scientists as the "heart brain." This system sends more signals to the brain than the brain sends to the heart.

When we experience fear, our heart rhythm becomes erratic and chaotic, disrupting our brain's higher functions.

When we experience love—or even appreciation—our heart rhythm becomes coherent and ordered, enhancing our brain's cognitive abilities.

In other words, fear makes us less intelligent. Love makes us more intelligent.

Which state would you rather make decisions from?

## RECOGNIZING FEAR-BASED PATTERNS IN BUSINESS

Fear shows up in business in predictable patterns:

- **Scarcity thinking**: *"There's not enough to go around."*
- **Comparison mindset**: *"We need to outdo our competitors."*
- **Perfectionism**: *"We can't launch until it's flawless."*
- **Control**: *"I need to micromanage to ensure quality."*
- **Short-term focus**: *"We need immediate results."*

These patterns might seem like "just good business sense." But look deeper and you'll recognize the energy of fear.

Fear constricts. Love expands.
Fear reacts. Love creates.
Fear protects. Love grows.

I've watched entrepreneurs make decisions from fear:

- Undercutting their prices (and their worth)
- Copying competitors instead of innovating
- Holding back their authentic voice for fear of rejection
- Overworking to the point of burnout

- Refusing to delegate or ask for help

The result? Businesses that drain rather than fulfill them. Growth that feels hollow rather than meaningful. Success that costs them their wellbeing.

## POWER VS. FORCE: THE HIDDEN MECHANISM

Earlier, we explored Hawkins' distinction between power and force. Now, let's deepen this understanding in the context of decision-making:

Fear-based decisions operate through force:

- Pushing for outcomes
- Fighting against circumstances
- Controlling for variables
- Resisting what is

Love-based decisions operate through power:

- Allowing for emergence
- Flowing with circumstances
- Co-creating with others
- Accepting what is before attempting to change it

Force diminishes over time and requires constant energy to maintain. Power is self-sustaining and actually grows through connection.

I experienced this distinction firsthand when launching my e-commerce business.

My first approach was force-based: I pushed for growth. I followed formulas rigidly. I fought against market limitations. I tried to control every outcome.

The result? Exhaustion. Limitation. Frustration.

When I embraced a power-based approach:

I allowed for organic growth.
I listened to my intuition.
I followed energy and enthusiasm.
I collaborated with circumstances.

The result? Expansion. Innovation. Flow.

Same business. Different energetic approach. Completely different outcome.

## THE "HOW WOULD LOVE RESPOND?" PRACTICE

When faced with any decision—from the seemingly insignificant to the strategically critical—try this simple practice:

1. **Notice the fear response:** Feel the contraction in your body. The narrowing of options. The urgency to react.
2. **Pause and breathe:** Create a space between the stimulus and the response. Just three deep breaths can recalibrate your entire nervous system.
3. **Ask the question:** *"How would love respond in this situation?"* Not sentimental love. Not passive love. Strategic, wisdom-filled, expansive love.
4. **Listen for the answer:** It often comes as a felt sense—a lightness, an opening, a clarity that emerges from your higher intelligence.
5. **Act from that guidance:** Move forward from what you've received, even if it differs from conventional wisdom.

I've applied this practice to:

- Hiring decisions
- Marketing strategy
- Product launches
- Client relationships
- Business partnerships

Each time, the love-based path revealed solutions that my fear-based thinking could never access.

## LOVE AS A STRATEGIC ADVANTAGE

In a world where businesses are increasingly automated, commoditized, and homogenized, leading with love isn't just ethical. It's strategic.

When you operate from higher frequencies:

- **You access greater creativity:** Fear narrows options. Love expands possibilities.
- **You build deeper loyalty:** Customers feel the difference in energy, even if they can't name it.
- **You create sustainable growth:** Force-based growth eventually collapses. Power-based growth compounds.
- **You attract aligned opportunities:** Your higher frequency naturally draws in similar energies.
- **You make better decisions:** With your full intelligence available, your choices become wiser.

Take Patagonia, a company that consistently chooses purpose over profit, even repairing customers' old gear rather than pushing them to buy new products. This love-based approach has created fanatical customer loyalty and a brand that stands apart in a crowded market.

Or consider the difference between Steve Jobs' first and second chapters at Apple. His early leadership relied heavily on force—control, perfectionism, and fear. His later leadership, while still demanding excellence, stemmed from a place of vision, purpose, and, yes, a love for what was possible. The results speak for themselves.

---

## 🌀 TRY THIS: FEAR TO LOVE TRANSLATION PRACTICE

Choose a current business challenge you're facing. First, write down your fear-based thoughts about it:

- What are you afraid might happen?
- What are you trying to control or avoid?
- Where do you feel constriction around this issue?

Now, translate each fear-based thought into a love-based alternative, as can be seen in the examples in table 22.1.

Notice how different each approach feels in your body.
Notice which thoughts expand your energy and which contract it.
Notice which thoughts generate fresh ideas and which ones shut down creativity.

This simple practice helps you recognize fear-based patterns and gently move toward love-based alternatives.

## TABLE 22.1 FEAR-BASED THINKING VS LOVE-BASED THINKING

| Fear-Based Thinking | Love-Based Thinking |
|---|---|
| "I need to watch every penny." | "I invest resources wisely to create maximum value." |
| "My competitor might steal my ideas." | "My unique energy cannot be duplicated." |
| "I need to hustle harder." | "I create from alignment and inspired action." |
| "What if this fails?" | "What can I learn, and how can I grow?" |

## OVERCOMING RESISTANCE TO LOVE-BASED LEADERSHIP

When I first share this concept with clients, I often hear:

*"But don't I need fear to motivate me?"*
*"Isn't love too soft for business?"*
*"What about tough decisions like firing someone?"*

These questions come from a misunderstanding of what love *really* is.

Love isn't weak. It's strong.
Love isn't blind. It's clear-seeing.
Love isn't always comfortable. It's always truthful.
Love-based leadership doesn't shy away from difficult decisions. It makes them from a place of clarity rather than reaction.

Letting go of team members who aren't aligned? Love does that—with compassion and respect.

Setting firm boundaries with clients? Love does that—with clarity and kindness.

Saying no to opportunities that don't fit? Love does that—with confidence and grace.

The difference isn't in *what* decisions are made. It's in the energy *from which* they're made.

## CLOSING REFLECTION: CHOOSING YOUR FREQUENCY

Every day, you stand at a crossroads. Every decision presents the same choice: Will you act from fear, or will you act from love?

The path of fear feels familiar. It masquerades as practicality. It promises safety.

But constriction is not safety. Limitation is not wisdom. Survival is not thriving.

The path of love feels expansive. It requires trust. It invites courage.

When you choose to operate from love, you access a higher intelligence. You align with the universal flow. You tap into limitless creativity.

Your business becomes not just a venture but a vehicle for purpose-driven growth.
Your decisions become not just strategic but enlightened.
Your leadership becomes not just effective but inspiring.

This change in consciousness—from fear to love—changes everything.

It's the difference between forcing an outcome and allowing something greater to emerge. Between pushing through resistance and flowing with aligned action. Between surviving in business and truly flourishing.

In the next chapter, we'll explore how this principle elevates your leadership—creating cultures of trust, innovation, and extraordinary engagement through heart-centered approaches.

But it all begins with this fundamental choice: In this moment, will you act from love, or will you act from fear?

The choice is always yours. And it changes everything.

# CHAPTER 23
# LEADING FROM THE HEART TO CREATE AUTHENTIC INFLUENCE

IF THERE'S one thing that's truly set my business apart, it's been relationships.

Not fancy systems. Not huge ad budgets. **Relationships**.

The kind that are built on trust. Honesty. Mutual respect.

And most of all— Open-heartedness.

From the very beginning, I approached business the same way I approach life: With genuine connection.

When I speak to my suppliers, I ask about their families. I check in on their holidays. I laugh with them. I also share parts of my personal life. Not as a strategy. Not to "win them over." But because that's how I move through the world. Because people come first.

And over the years, that heart-first approach has created something meaningful: Loyalty. Trust. Support that goes both ways.

I once had a contractor working with me say, "I've never seen anything like the relationships you have with your suppliers."

He was amazed at the terms I was offered, even as a small business. Amazed at how they prioritized my orders ahead of massive multinational clients. Why? Because I didn't just show up as a "customer." I showed up as a person.

## THE UNSEEN CURRENCY OF BUSINESS

What many overlook in the rush to optimize and scale is that business runs on an invisible currency: relationship capital.

This isn't just warm, fuzzy feelings. It's a tangible asset with real-world impact. When supply chains tightened during global disruptions, my products still shipped. When materials became scarce, my suppliers set some aside. Not because I had the biggest orders but because we had cultivated genuine relationships.

The same principle extends to team dynamics. In a digital landscape where turnover is high and loyalty often feels transactional, my core team has stayed for years. They go above and beyond—not out of obligation but because I treat them with compassion and respect.

I understand that they're not just employees or VAs. They're whole humans. With families. With dreams. With lives beyond the screen.

One team member in the Philippines was facing a family health crisis. Instead of just offering sympathetic words, we restructured her schedule and sent additional support. The result? Not only did she stay with us through a difficult time, but her commitment to our mission deepened. This wasn't calculated—it was simply the right thing to do.

This is where heart-centered leadership becomes a strategic advantage: when you invest in people as people, they invest in your vision as their own.

## APPLYING LOVE-BASED DECISION-MAKING TO LEADERSHIP

In the previous chapter, we explored how acting from love rather than fear elevates our decision-making and creates more aligned, meaningful outcomes. Now, let's see how this principle reshapes one of the most impactful areas of business: leadership.

Traditional leadership often teaches: Don't mix business with emotion. Don't show weakness. Keep it professional.

But what if that old model is what's *broken*?

What if it's not about removing emotion— but becoming more emotionally *attuned*?

What if true leadership isn't about having all the answers— but knowing how to listen, reflect, and respond with love?

When we bring the love-based decision-making framework into leadership, we naturally access the power that Hawkins describes rather than relying on force. Stepping into this way of leading asks for something often discouraged in traditional business: vulnerability.

When we've hit tough times, I've shared that with my team. I've said, "Things are challenging right now. But I believe in what we're building. And I believe in us."

When something has gone wrong, I haven't come in with blame. I've asked, "What are your thoughts? What can we learn from this together?"

And in those moments, our bond deepened. Because when people feel *seen*, they show up differently.

Research from Harvard Business Review underscores something I've seen firsthand: vulnerability in leadership doesn't diminish authority—it enhances it. Leaders who openly share their challenges and acknowledge when they don't have all the answers are perceived as more authentic and trustworthy (HBR, 2022).

This perspective aligns with Brené Brown's extensive work on daring leadership, where she emphasizes that embracing vulnerability is foundational to courageous and effective leadership (Brown, 2018). By leaning into vulnerability, leaders foster deeper connections and cultivate environments of trust and innovation.

True heart-centered leadership means:

- Communicating your desires and boundaries with compassion
- Receiving feedback without defensiveness
- Celebrating others freely
- Admitting when you don't know
- Choosing curiosity over control

And above all: ***Showing up fully human.***

Because when you do, you give others permission to do the same.

Heart-centered leadership isn't soft. It's strong.

It builds cultures of trust and innovation. It fosters loyalty you can't buy. It opens the door to deeper collaboration, creativity, and resilience.

## THE BALANCE OF HEART AND STRUCTURE

One of the biggest myths we're still breaking down is that business must be separate from humanity—that professionalism and emotion can't coexist.

But what's often forgotten is this: When business becomes too rigid, too sterile— it loses its soul.

Business *is* personal. Because **business is built on relationships**.

This doesn't mean abandoning systems or clarity. In fact, heart-centered leadership requires a thoughtful balance of structure and flexibility, firmness and compassion.

In my business, we have clear expectations, detailed SOPs, and accountability measures. But we hold these structures with humanity, understanding that life happens and adaptation is part of the journey.

This balance shows up in how we:

- **Set clear boundaries with compassion**: "I value your input tremendously. For me to give it the attention it deserves, I need it by Thursday."
- **Provide feedback with care**: "This approach isn't aligned with our goals, and I believe you have the creativity to take it in a stronger direction. Let's explore some alternatives."
- **Navigate conflict with openness**: "I noticed tension in our last meeting. I'd love to understand your perspective better so we can move forward together."

You can be kind and still be clear. You can be vulnerable and still be strong. You can be warm and still make bold decisions.

The key is that structure exists to support the humans within it—not to constrain them. When people understand the "why" behind the "what," engagement rises naturally.

## THE RIPPLE EFFECT OF LEADING WITH LOVE

When you show up as your whole self in business, the impact extends far beyond your immediate team. It creates a ripple effect that touches every aspect of your business ecosystem.

I witnessed this with an e-commerce client who had built her business on rigorous efficiency and distance. Her team delivered adequate results, but innovation was stagnant. Turnover was high. When she began implementing heart-centered leadership practices—regular check-ins focused on both work and wellbeing, transparent communication about business challenges, celebration of individual contributions—the entire energy of the team began to evolve.

Within six months, her team began proactively solving problems they previously would have escalated. Creative ideas flowed more freely. And when a major launch faced unexpected obstacles, her team rallied with solutions instead of complaints.

The revenue impact was significant, but what moved her most was this feedback from a team member: "For the first time, I feel like I'm building something meaningful, not just doing tasks."

The impact of this evolution extends beyond your team. It influences:

- **Client relationships**: They deepen into partnerships where both sides invest more fully
- **Marketplace reputation**: Word-of-mouth referrals increase when people feel genuinely valued
- **Brand identity**: Your business becomes known not just for what you sell, but how you show up

You create cultures where people feel safe to share ideas. Where feedback is a gift—not a threat. Where failure isn't punished—but mined for wisdom.

And you inspire loyalty—not by force, but through connection.

I've seen this pattern repeat time and again, not just in my own business, but in the lives of the women I mentor.

When they surrender the armour and speak from their truth, connection deepens—and everything begins to flow.

## 🌀 TRY THIS: THE HEART-CENTERED LEADERSHIP CHECK-IN

This simple practice can redefine how you show up as a leader. Schedule 10 minutes with yourself at least once a week:

**1. Energy Assessment:** Ask yourself:

- Am I leading from fear or from love?
- Where am I withholding honesty because I'm afraid of how I'll be perceived?
- What would it look like to lead with both strength and softness?

**2. Relationship Review:** Consider one key relationship in your business (team member, client, partner):

- Have I truly seen this person beyond their role?
- What might they need that they haven't expressed?
- How can I create more safety for authentic connection?

**3. Courageous Action:** Based on your reflections, commit to one action:

- Have the honest conversation you've been avoiding
- Express specific appreciation for someone's contribution
- Share a challenge you're facing and ask for input
- Be a little more you, with the people who matter

The power of this check-in isn't just in the reflection—it's in the consistent action that follows.

## CLOSING REFLECTION: THE POWER OF HUMAN-CENTERED BUSINESS

You don't need to be a hard-ass to lead well. You don't need to keep your heart out of the boardroom.

You just need to lead with love.

Your business is not just a brand. It's an **energetic extension of you**.

When I first started implementing these principles, I worried I might be perceived as "soft" or "unprofessional." What I discovered instead was that authenticity became my competitive advantage. In a world of automated responses and transactional relationships, genuine human connection stands out.

Heart-centered leadership isn't just about being nice. It's about applying those higher vibrational frequencies we discussed in the previous chapter to your role as a leader. It's about creating businesses that honor the full humanity of everyone involved—and in doing so, building enterprises that are more resilient, innovative, and ultimately, successful.

When you lead with open-heartedness, authenticity, and care, you create more than transactions—you create transformation.

And that ripple? It goes further than you think.

From your team to your customers. From your vendors to your community. From your daily operations to your legacy.

This is the essence of *Ready to Rise:* When you lead from your heart, you don't just build a business. You create a movement.

## CHAPTER 24
# FEELING IT FIRST: HOW SOULPRENEURS MANIFEST BUSINESS RESULTS THROUGH EMOTIONAL ALIGNMENT

LET'S BE HONEST.

We're often taught to chase the "what"—the income, the title, the lifestyle, the six-figure launch. But rarely are we asked:

*"How do you want to feel?"*

Because behind every goal is a feeling we're hoping to experience once we get there: Freedom. Peace. Confidence. Fulfillment.

But what if we didn't wait? What if we started creating our lives *from* those feelings—right now?

This shift—from pursuing external achievements to generating internal states—is at the heart of living your most authentic life.

## THE NEUROSCIENCE OF EMOTIONAL MANIFESTATION

This approach isn't just inspirational philosophy. It's rooted in cutting-edge neuroscience and quantum physics.

As Dispenza's research shows, your thoughts create electromagnetic signals, while your emotions generate magnetic ones. Together, they form your energetic signature that communicates with the quantum field around you.

When you consistently operate from lower emotional frequencies—frustration, fear, anxiety, or lack—you create a neurochemical state that reinforces these feelings, making them your default experience. Your brain becomes wired to notice evidence that supports this emotional baseline.

But here's the revolutionary understanding: You can *consciously* change this frequency.

When you elevate your emotional state through gratitude, joy, or self-love, you create new neural pathways that fundamentally change your perception and what you attract. You're rewiring your brain to experience your desired reality before it physically manifests.

As Dispenza explains: "Your brain doesn't know the difference between an experience that's happening in your outer world and an experience that's happening in your inner world." When you embody the emotional state of your future self now, your brain processes it as if it were reality.

This isn't "fake it till you make it." It's neurologically *becoming* it.

## CREATING YOUR EMOTIONAL VISION BOARD

Understanding this science alters how we approach manifestation tools, such as vision boards.

Traditional vision boards often focus on outer results, such as houses, cars, and vacation destinations.

I invite you to create an emotional vision board instead:

- What words describe how you want to feel? (Sovereign, peaceful, vibrant, creative, abundant)
- What images evoke these feelings for you?
- What colors align with these emotional states?
- What quotes or affirmations support these feelings?

Place this somewhere you'll see it daily, and let it remind you that your desired feelings are available now—not after achieving some future milestone.

This approach reimagines a vision board from a wishlist into a frequency activator—a daily reminder of the emotional states you're choosing to embody now.

## SELF-LOVE AS YOUR AUTHENTIC FOUNDATION

For this emotional approach to manifestation to work, it must be built on a foundation of self-love.

Not the superficial kind. The fierce kind. The kind that says:

*"I matter—whether I'm visibly succeeding or quietly resting."*
*"I trust myself—even when the path isn't clear."*
*"I'm not here to perform for anyone. I'm here to be who I truly am."*

I learned this lesson the hard way. After achieving what seemed like success in my business, I still felt the same insecurities and the same need for validation. The accomplishments didn't fix anything—they just temporarily masked my lack of self-love.

In my book, *A Scientific Approach To Rewiring Self-Love*, I unpack how true inner work begins when we understand that our outer world will always mirror our inner relationship with ourselves. The frequency of self-doubt can never attract the life that self-love creates.

Self-love is recognizing that you already are what you've been seeking. You are already worthy of everything you desire—not because of what you do but because of who you are at your core. This understanding of neuroplasticity, combined with practical self-love exercises outlined in my book, creates a strong foundation for manifesting your authentic life.

Brené Brown calls this "true belonging"—the practice of belonging so deeply to yourself that external approval becomes secondary to your own truth.

From that place of self-belonging, you become magnetic. You become free. You stop shape-shifting to be validated and start standing in your wholeness.

## PRACTICAL MANIFESTATION: THE FEELING-FIRST APPROACH

With this foundation of self-love, you're ready to implement one of the deepest insights I've embodied in my journey:

You don't manifest what you want—you manifest *what you are*.

If your goals emerge from love, peace, and purpose, you'll attract opportunities that match that energy. This is why so many "successful" people remain unfulfilled. They've achieved outer targets without addressing the emotional states driving their pursuits.

The solution is simple but profound: Don't wait to feel how you want to feel. Create those feelings now.

When you consciously generate the emotional state of your desired reality, you initiate what Dispenza refers to as "the quantum law of creation." You're no longer trying to get somewhere to feel something—you're feeling it first and letting physical reality catch up to your internal state.

## YOUR EMOTIONAL CREATION PRACTICE

Here's a daily practice to begin living from your desired feelings:

1. **Morning Embodiment**: Before checking emails or social media, sit quietly and ask, *"How do I want to feel today?"* Then, consciously generate that feeling in your body. Notice where it lives physically. Breathe into it. Amplify it.
2. **Emotional Clarity in Decision-Making:** Before making any significant decision, pause and ask: *"What feeling am I trying to create with this choice?"* Then ask: *"Is this choice aligned with my desired emotional state?"*
3. **Evening Celebration**: Each night, acknowledge moments when you successfully generated your desired feelings, regardless of external circumstances. These moments are reprogramming your nervous system.

For those who wish to delve deeper into this practice, consider exploring Dispenza's meditation techniques. His work includes various forms of meditation—sitting, standing, walking, and lying down—designed to help you cultivate heart-brain coherence and embody the energy of your future self. Through these practices, you can learn to generate and sustain elevated emotional states, creating a new electromagnetic signature that draws your desired reality toward you.

This practice isn't about ignoring challenges or pretending everything is perfect. It's about consciously choosing your emotional home base, rather than letting circumstances dictate it.

## ✺ TRY THIS: DESIRED FEELINGS INVENTORY

1. Write down your top 3 goals right now.
2. Next to each one, ask: *"What do I believe this will make me feel?"*
3. For each feeling identified, close your eyes and recall a time when you've experienced this feeling, even if only briefly.
4. Notice the physical sensations associated with this feeling. Where do you feel it in your body?
5. Practice generating this feeling for 2-3 minutes daily, independent of achieving the goal.
6. Journal about how this practice begins affecting your experience.

You'll be amazed how quickly life responds when you lead with energy instead of effort.

As Dispenza's research confirms, when your thoughts align with elevated emotion over time, you broadcast a new electromagnetic signature that draws your future self toward you.

---

## CLOSING REFLECTION: FROM EXTERNAL VALIDATION TO INTERNAL ALIGNMENT

You were never meant to hustle your way into peace. You were meant to align with it.

Living your most authentic life means taking the focus from what the world expects to how you *want to feel*.

When self-love becomes your foundation,
When emotional resonance becomes your roadmap,

When choosing your frequency becomes your daily practice—
You stop chasing. You start creating.
And you become a woman who leads her life from the inside out.

In the next chapter, we'll explore how intuition becomes even more accessible when your inner world is coherent and emotionally clear.

Because when you live from truth, you begin to hear your inner guidance again.

And that changes ***everything***.

## CHAPTER 25
# INTUITIVE INTELLIGENCE: TRUSTING THE INNER GUIDANCE THAT BUILDS ALIGNED SUCCESS

WE LIVE in a world that teaches us to seek answers outside ourselves.

To validate. To compare. To perform.
But there's a quieter wisdom within you.
And it's been speaking to you all along.

You may know it as instinct, a gut feeling, or an inner nudge. You may feel it in your body before you can explain it in words.

This is your intuition.

And when you begin to clear the noise—of conditioning, fear, and distraction—you begin to hear it again.

## RELEARNING TO TRUST WHAT YOU KNOW

As children, we're deeply intuitive.

We choose who to trust without being told. We follow joy without needing permission. We cry when something feels wrong and light up when it feels right.

But somewhere along the way, we learn to doubt ourselves.

To override the "yes" in our bellies or the "no" in our chest.

To rationalize. To minimize. To disconnect.

This chapter is about returning to that innate intelligence— not just for personal clarity, but for leadership, for creation, and for your business success.

Because when your inner guidance is strong, your outer world starts aligning.

## INTUITION VS. TRIGGER

Let's be clear: not everything that feels urgent is intuition.

Sometimes, what we think is "a sign" is actually a trigger.

So, how do we distinguish between them?

Intuition is calm. Neutral. It whispers.
Triggers are charged. Loud. They demand.
One arises from wisdom. The other from wounds.

This distinction is crucial for entrepreneurs who must make decisions daily that impact their businesses and lives.

When something comes up—pause.

Ask yourself: *"Is this a quiet knowing or a loud reaction?"*

Am I being guided by something true and timeless within me? Or am I reacting to something unresolved?

With practice, the difference becomes unmistakable, enabling you to make decisions based on clarity rather than reaction.

## THE GUT-BRAIN CONNECTION: YOUR BODY KNOWS

Science backs this up, revealing why gut instincts matter in business and life.

The "gut feeling" isn't just a metaphor—it's biological.

The gut has its own complex neural network, often called the "second brain." It contains over 100 million neurons—more than in your spinal cord. The gut communicates with the brain via the vagus nerve, playing a huge role in emotional regulation and intuitive decision-making.

Neuroscientist Antonio Damasio's research reveals that our bodies often sense what's right before our conscious minds catch up. In *The Feeling of What Happens*, he explains that these bodily sensations, or "somatic markers," are emotional signals that guide our decisions and behaviors. Far from being mere feelings, they represent a deeper intelligence that supports our survival, fosters creativity, and drives personal growth (Damasio, 1999).

When we learn to interpret these signals accurately, we begin making decisions that are not only more aligned with our authentic purpose but often far more effective than those driven purely by logic. This is why some of the world's most successful entrepreneurs attribute their most significant breakthroughs to their gut instincts.

## THE INTUITIVE GAP: WHERE MOST ENTREPRENEURS STRUGGLE

Many successful business owners hit a ceiling not because of a lack of strategy, but because they've disconnected from their intuitive guidance. They've learned to override their inner knowing with:

- "Expert" advice that doesn't feel right
- Data that contradicts their deeper understanding of their market
- Social pressure to follow conventional paths
- Fear of being seen as "irrational" or "woo-woo"

What sets truly extraordinary entrepreneurs apart is their ability to strike a balance between analytical thinking and intuitive wisdom. They recognize that both are essential, complementary tools.

As I explored in my book *A Scientific Approach To Rewiring Self-Love*, this balance becomes easier to achieve when you establish a foundation of self-trust. When you genuinely value your own internal guidance system, you become less susceptible to external pressures and more attuned to what actually serves your business.

## FOLLOWING THE BREADCRUMBS

Once you reconnect with your intuition, you start to notice the breadcrumbs.

You know the ones...

A book falls off the shelf with the exact information you need for your next launch.

A conversation with a stranger presents the perfect opportunity for a joint venture.

An idea arrives during meditation that solves the problem your team has been wrestling with for weeks.

Coincidence? Maybe. But what if it's something more?

Carl Jung introduced the concept of *synchronicity* to describe meaningful coincidences that lack a clear causal relationship yet feel profoundly significant (Jung, 1960). These events often seem random to the logical mind, but on a deeper level, they suggest an underlying order to our experiences.

For me, breadcrumbs are the universe's way of guiding us—subtle signs pointing us toward greater alignment, even when the path isn't obvious. They are the arrows, the nudges, the gentle invitations to respond, explore, or pay attention.

In my entrepreneurial journey, these breadcrumbs have appeared more frequently the more I've trusted myself. They've led to pivotal business relationships, innovative product ideas, and perfect timing for launches I couldn't have planned if I tried.

The thing about breadcrumbs is: they don't scream.

They whisper.
They nudge.
They invite.

And sometimes, we miss them, especially when we're rigidly focused on the way we think things *should* unfold. If we're too attached to our own plans, we can overlook the signs that a better path is trying to reveal itself.

To follow them requires presence, openness, and a willingness to trust what doesn't always make sense on paper, but feels deeply aligned with your vision.

Because sometimes the universe is showing you the way—you just have to be willing to see it.

## NOTHING IS RANDOM: THE INTELLIGENCE BEHIND BUSINESS "LUCK"

When you begin living from this place, where inner guidance meets external congruence, your business begins to flow with greater ease and clarity.

You stop needing to control everything.
You stop demanding certainty before you move.
And instead, you begin dancing with the mystery.

Believing that nothing is random opens you to a new way of leading:

Every client interaction.
Every market shift.
Every "coincidence" becomes an opportunity to listen more closely to what's unfolding

This is where business becomes magical.
This is where entrepreneurship becomes art.
This is where purpose meets profit.

Have you noticed how often successful business owners seem to be "in the right place at the right time"? What appears as luck to others is frequently this intuitive intelligence at work—guiding them to opportunities others miss.

## INTUITION IN BUSINESS: YOUR COMPETITIVE EDGE

Many of my most pivotal business decisions haven't come from spreadsheets—they've come from stillness.

From a felt sense that something was aligned... or not.

Whether I was assessing a supplier relationship, considering a new hire, or walking away from a shiny opportunity that didn't feel right, my intuition was the differentiator.

In my e-commerce business, I've made inventory decisions that seemed counterintuitive on paper but resulted in our most successful product launches. I've trusted hiring choices based partly on a "feeling" about someone, who then became an invaluable team member.

In the fast-paced world of entrepreneurship, logic is necessary. But intuition is what sets the visionary apart from the merely strategic.

The more you cultivate inner stillness, the louder that wisdom becomes.

And the more you trust it, the more unwavering and precise it becomes.

## CREATING SPACE FOR INTUITIVE INTELLIGENCE

For the achievement-oriented entrepreneur, slowing down to listen inwardly can feel counterproductive. However, the most innovative business leaders understand that intuitive insights often arrive precisely when we step away from constant doing.

What's truly happening in these moments is the essential balancing of feminine and masculine energies. As I've mentioned earlier, in our business culture, we often overindex on masculine energy—the driving, achieving, analytical force that pushes forward.

While this energy is vital for execution, it's the feminine energy—receptive, intuitive, and flowing—that allows our intuition to speak clearly.

It's specifically in this feminine space that intuition becomes accessible. When we consciously create balance between these complementary energies, we tap back into our natural intuitive wisdom. The masculine provides structure and implementation, while the feminine offers insight and intuitive flow. Together, they create a powerful entrepreneurial approach that integrates both strategy and intuition.

Here are three practices that have helped me and my clients strengthen intuitive intelligence by honoring this balance:

**1. Decision-Free Mornings:** Reserve the first 30-60 minutes of your day for presence rather than productivity. Before checking emails or planning your day, take a moment to simply be. This creates an opportunity for intuitive insights about your business to emerge naturally.

**2. Body-Mind Check-Ins:** Before making significant business decisions, consciously check in with your body. Notice any sensations, tensions, or expansions. Your body often registers alignment or misalignment before your mind can articulate it.

**3. Regular Digital Detox:** Schedule periodic breaks from digital inputs—even just a few hours. These information fasts clear mental clutter, allowing your natural intuition to speak more clearly about your business direction.

---

## ⊚ TRY THIS: INTUITION RECONNECTION PRACTICE FOR ENTREPRENEURS

Sit quietly. Breathe deeply.

Bring to mind a business decision or question you're facing.

Ask yourself: *"What does my intuition say about this?"*

Notice where you feel the response in your body. Is it tight? Expansive? Clear? Clouded?

Without forcing an answer, just listen. Be with the sensation.

Then, journal what came through, noting both the logical considerations and the intuitive guidance.

Trust may not come all at once. But the signal will strengthen with time and practice.

---

## CLOSING REFLECTION: YOUR INNER COMPASS FOR BUSINESS AND LIFE

You were born with everything you need to navigate both life and business.

You are not lost.
You are not behind.
You simply forgot to listen for the guidance that's been whispering all along.

Your intuition is a compass.

Not one that shouts from the outside—but one that hums quietly from within.

Let it lead you.

Because your next groundbreaking offer, your next aligned client, your next business breakthrough?

**It begins with trusting yourself.**

In the next chapter, we'll explore how to turn these intuitive insights into concrete action steps that move your business forward while honoring your authentic vision.

## CHAPTER 26
# SOUL LEGACY: CREATING IMPACT THAT ECHOES BEYOND YOUR LIFETIME

WHAT WILL you be remembered for?

Legacy isn't reserved for the famous or the few. It's not about buildings named after you or bank accounts left behind. Legacy is what people feel because you existed. It's the energy you brought to the room, the values you stood for, the courage you modelled when you chose a different way.

It's every moment you decided to live in alignment with your truth—even when it defied the expectations of others.

For most of my life, I followed the rules. I didn't question them—I just assumed that doing what was expected was the right thing to do. I ticked all the boxes, played the part, and waited for fulfillment to arrive with my gold stars.

But it never came.

Even when I was "successful," I still felt an emptiness I couldn't explain. Something within me whispered that I wasn't living my own life—I was living someone else's version of it.

## THE MOMENT EVERYTHING CHANGED

The breakthrough didn't happen in a journal or during a meditation. It happened in real life—mid-conversation.

Someone looked at me and said, "But you can't do that." And without missing a beat, I responded:

*"According to whose rules?"*

That wasn't rehearsed. It came straight from the part of me that was finally waking up. That question marked the moment I stopped blindly following and started consciously choosing.

Until then, I had done all the "right" things—followed the formulas, ticked the boxes, met the expectations. I was living the life I was taught to want. But deep down, I felt disconnected, as if I were moving through someone else's version of success.

It wasn't until I began challenging those inherited beliefs that I realized:

Following the rules doesn't guarantee fulfillment. *But honoring what's real for you often does.*

## THE ENTREPRENEUR'S LEGACY DILEMMA

As entrepreneurs, we face a unique legacy challenge. We've often broken away from conventional careers, yet we may still be carrying conventional definitions of success.

We left the world of being an employee to escape someone else's rules, only to impose equally rigid expectations on ourselves. We chase metrics that don't align with our values—revenue targets disconnected from impact, growth that sacrifices well-being, or visibility that comes at the cost of genuine connection.

I've worked with several business owners who built "successful" companies only to realize they'd created beautifully decorated prisons. Their businesses demanded conformity rather than expressing their authentic vision.

The most painful legacy failure is not building something that fails—it's creating something that succeeds but doesn't matter to you.

This is why legacy work isn't a luxury for entrepreneurs—it's an essential strategy. When your business reflects your true values, you create something sustainable, not just financially, but also emotionally and spiritually.

## FIVE STEPS TO CHALLENGING NORMS AND CREATING YOUR TRUE LEGACY

If you're ready to create a legacy that reflects who you truly are—not who you've been taught to be—start here:

**1. Awaken to the Narrative**

Become aware of the beliefs, expectations, and societal scripts that have shaped your decisions. These include messages you inherited about success, gender, worth, work, relationships, and leadership.

**Legacy Practice:** Take inventory of the "rules" you follow in your business. For each one, ask: "Where did this rule come from? Does it actually serve my highest vision?"

Pay particular attention to the rules that feel non-negotiable—these are often the most limiting and least questioned.

**2. Question Everything**

Ask yourself:

- Who told me this was true?

- Is this my value or someone else's?
- What would I choose if I weren't afraid of judgment?

The goal isn't to rebel for rebellion's sake—it's to discern what's truly aligned with your higher self.

**Legacy Practice:** Identify one "best practice" in your industry that feels restrictive or inauthentic to you. Challenge yourself to consider an alternative approach that would feel more aligned.

Remember that the most influential leaders throughout history didn't follow best practices—they created them.

### 3. Choose Integrity Over Approval

Choosing a path that honors your soul might disappoint people who benefit from your compliance. Do it anyway. Integrity isn't about being liked—it's about being whole.

Every authentic business decision will likely face resistance—from competitors comfortable with the status quo, from audiences resistant to change, and sometimes even from team members.

**Legacy Practice:** Identify one area where you've been compromising your vision to maintain approval. Create a plan to realign this area with your true values.

This step requires courage but also compassion—for yourself and others. Change creates waves, and not everyone will appreciate the disruption.

### 4. Redefine Success on Your Terms

Let go of narrow definitions of success. You get to define what a meaningful business looks like. Maybe it's scaling a company or maintaining a boutique practice. Maybe it's living slowly, creatively, and intentionally. There is no one right way—only your way.

In my own journey, redefining success meant recognizing that my highest value wasn't exponential growth but meaningful impact. That redefinition impacted everything, from my pricing to my team structure.

**Legacy Practice:** Write your own success metrics. Beyond revenue, what would truly represent success in alignment with your values? Consider metrics like:

- The depth of breakthroughs your clients experience
- The sustainability of your business model
- The authenticity of your marketing
- The joy you feel in your daily work

When you measure what truly matters to you, you create a business that reflects your authentic legacy.

**5. Live It Loudly**

When you choose to live by your own truth, you give others permission to do the same. Your courage becomes a blueprint for others who are still afraid to color outside the lines.

**Legacy Practice:** Identify one way you can make your values more visible in your business this month. This might be through:

- A transparent message about a difficult decision
- A policy change that better reflects your principles
- A new offering that addresses an overlooked need
- A boundary you set with clients or partners

Your most authentic legacy often emerges from these moments of visible clear connection between your values and your actions.

## CHOICE: THE SACRED POWER WE FORGET WE HAVE

Choice is where your legacy is born—not in grand gestures, but in the quiet, consistent moments when you pause and ask:

*Is this what I really believe?*
*Is this choice aligned with my values, or just familiar?*
*Am I reacting from an old wound or responding from my highest self?*

As Viktor Frankl famously said:

> "Between stimulus and response, there is a space. In that space is our power to choose our response. In our response lies our growth and our freedom."

That space—the sacred pause—is where everything shifts.

And neuroscience confirms this. As I explore in my book *"A Scientific Approach To Rewiring Self-Love,"* every time we override our automatic programming and choose differently, we change the structure of our brain. We weaken the neural pathways of old habits and strengthen new ones.

In that pause, your brain rewires.
In that pause, your future begins.

This isn't just personal development. It's personal liberation. Choosing to respond differently is how we step off the hamster wheel of self-sabotage and onto the path of conscious creation.

## YOUR BUSINESS AS A LEGACY VEHICLE

Your business isn't separate from your legacy—it can be a vehicle for creating it. Every policy, offering, marketing message, and client interaction either reinforces conventional thinking or challenges it with something more authentic.

Consider how your business might:

- Challenge industry norms that don't serve people
- Create more inclusive models of success
- Demonstrate values-driven decision making
- Prioritize sustainability over short-term gains
- Center wellbeing alongside productivity
- Serve as a vehicle for philanthropy—integrating social impact into your business model to support causes aligned with your values

The entrepreneurial journey offers daily opportunities to choose what feels true over what's expected. Each choice shapes not only your business but the mark you leave on your world.

Don't wait until "someday" to consider your legacy. It's being written right now with every choice you make. The question isn't whether you'll leave a legacy—it's whether that legacy will be intentional or accidental.

---

## 🌀 TRY THIS: LEGACY INVENTORY & DECLARATION

Take a moment to connect with your inner wisdom. Journal on the following:

- What inherited "rules" or expectations have I been living by that no longer feel aligned?
- Where in my life or business am I still waiting for permission?

- What is one bold choice I could make this week that reflects the legacy I want to leave?
- If my business were a message to the world, what would I want it to say?
- How can I use my voice, energy, or platform to challenge the status quo for good?

Then, craft a one-sentence personal manifesto. Let it reflect the values you're choosing to live by—not the one you inherited.

*"I am a woman who dares to live fully, love deeply, and lead boldly—on my terms."*

Write it. Speak it. Post it. Let it become your compass.

## CLOSING REFLECTION: THE COURAGE TO CREATE YOUR OWN PATH

Creating a legacy isn't about grand gestures.

It's about quiet courage. Moment-by-moment choices. The willingness to stand in your truth when it would be easier to conform.

The world doesn't need more carbon copies of past success stories. It needs your voice. Your perspective. Your way of doing things.

No formula can guide you here. No roadmap exists for your unique path.

It's forged in those moments when you pause and ask:

*What if I trusted myself completely?*
*What if I stopped asking for permission?*
*What if I created my own rules?*

Your legacy emerges when you stop asking *"What should I do?"* and start declaring, *"This is what I'm here to create."*

This shift—from external validation to internal guidance—changes everything.

Every time you choose truth over tradition... Inner wisdom over external validation... Courage over comfort...

You are building your legacy. Right here. Right now.

In the next chapter, we'll explore how to translate this legacy vision into practical systems that support sustainable growth while honoring your deepest values.

# CHAPTER 27
# THE SOULPRENEUR'S PATH: YOUR NEW BLUEPRINT FOR LIVING, LEADING, AND RISING

**THIS IS NOT THE END.** It's the beginning. The moment you stop chasing strategies and start living from your soul. The moment you stop asking *"What should I do?"* and start asking, *"Who am I here to be?"*

This is the path of the Soulpreneur.

We've traveled together through healing, awareness, alignment, and awakening. We've explored what it means to lead from the inside out. And now, everything converges here: the place where purpose meets practice, where being informs doing, and where your inner work becomes the source of your outer impact.

You didn't pick up this book because you were looking for another business blueprint. You picked it up because you felt something stir. A knowing that there's more to success than metrics. More to leadership than performance. More to you than what the world sees.

And you were right.

## WHAT IT MEANS TO BE A SOULPRENEUR

A Soulpreneur is a woman who no longer separates her personal growth from her professional path.

She builds from within.
She leads with integrity.
She allows her intuition to be just as valid as her spreadsheet.

Being a Soulpreneur isn't about a niche. It's about a *frequency*.

She trusts that her inner alignment is her strategy. That her energy is her magnetism. That her purpose is more than a tagline—it's the why behind everything she creates.

She knows that the most important question is not, *"What should I sell?"* but rather, *"What am I here to embody?"*

This path isn't about reaching a destination. It's about deepening into who you are and allowing that presence to shape your business, your relationships, and your legacy.

## SOUL PURPOSE: YOUR ULTIMATE COMPASS

Every woman I've mentored who's burned out or stuck at a plateau has one thing in common: She's disconnected from her deeper "why."

Not the clever one she puts on her website—but the soul-level one.

Your soul purpose isn't found by copying someone else's model. It's remembered through stillness, honesty, and inner attunement. It rises when you choose to honour your inner knowing over external expectations. When you follow the breadcrumbs of joy. When you honour your boundaries, voice, and vision—even when it feels risky.

Your soul purpose is your true north. It's what you were born to offer the world. Not through effort but through embodiment.

When your purpose leads, everything else flows. Clarity sharpens. Creativity expands. Clients feel the difference because you're no longer selling from a script. You're leading from a frequency.

## UNCOVERING YOUR SOUL PURPOSE

Many entrepreneurs struggle with identifying their soul purpose. They've been running businesses based on market demand or expert advice rather than inner calling. Others have a sense of their purpose but haven't fully claimed it or allowed it to lead their business decisions.

This disconnection shows up as:

- Offering services that drain rather than energize you
- Feeling like you're wearing a mask in your marketing
- Success that leaves you oddly empty
- Constantly searching for the "right" business model

Your soul purpose isn't something you invent—it's something you uncover. It exists at the intersection of your natural gifts, your deepest values, and the service that makes your heart sing.

---

## ◉ TRY THIS: SOUL PURPOSE DISCOVERY JOURNEY

Take a reflective journey through these questions. Move through them slowly, allowing your intuition rather than your strategic mind to guide your answers:

1. **Your Natural State of Being**
   - When do you lose track of time?
   - What were you naturally drawn to as a child before the world told you who to be?
   - What qualities do others consistently recognize in you?
   - What feels like breathing to you but seems like a superpower to others?
2. **Your Highest Values**
   - What matters most to you in how you live each day?
   - What would you stand for even if it wasn't popular?
   - What do you want to be remembered for?
   - What makes you feel most alive?
3. **Your Service Alignment**
   - What problems do you solve with natural ease?
   - Whose growth journey has deeply moved you?
   - What form of contribution leaves you feeling energized rather than depleted?
   - What would you help with even if you weren't paid?
4. **Your Emotional Resonance**
   - What brings you to tears (in a good way)?
   - What injustice or gap in the world can you not ignore?
   - What do you find yourself constantly learning about?
   - What message do you keep receiving that you're meant to share?

From these reflections, look for patterns and resonant themes. Your soul purpose often lives in the overlap of these different dimensions.

Now, craft a soul purpose statement beginning with "I believe my purpose is to..."

This isn't about perfection—it's about resonance. Does it feel true in your body? Does it bring a sense of both peace and excitement? Does it feel bigger than just your business?

This statement becomes your north star, guiding decisions from product creation to client selection to marketing messages. It's not about what you do—it's about who you are being while you do it.

---

## THE RIPPLE OF BECOMING

When you live from soul alignment, it doesn't just transform your business—it transforms the world around you.

Your courage to be fully yourself liberates others to do the same. Your healing creates safer spaces for others to grow. Your authenticity becomes your brand. Your presence becomes your leadership. And your life—exactly as it is—is the message.

You don't have to be perfect. You just have to be present. Because who you are is the real offering.

I've witnessed this kind of inner change ripple through people more many times. When entrepreneurs stop compartmentalizing their "business selves" from their "real selves," everything changes. One client completely reimagined her coaching practice after reconnecting with her childhood love of storytelling. Another simplified her entire business model to align with her deep value of presence, cutting her offerings in half but doubling her impact and revenue.

These weren't just strategic pivots—they were soul alignments. And they didn't require massive action plans. They simply needed the courage to let their being inform their doing.

## THIS IS NOT YOUR TYPICAL BUSINESS BOOK

This book was never intended to provide a list of things to do. It was written to remind you of who you already are.

You don't need to be fixed. You don't need another guru. You need your own truth, trusted and lived.

When you begin to walk the Soulpreneur's Path, business becomes a living, breathing expression of your inner world.

It becomes art.
It becomes medicine.
It becomes a mirror.

And you? **You become unstoppable**—not because of strategy but because of you're *living in integrity with your soul.*

Consider how this path differs from conventional business approaches:

**Conventional Business Logic vs. Soulpreneur Wisdom**

Where conventional business says, "Find a profitable niche," the Soulpreneur asks, *"What am I naturally drawn to serve?"*

Where conventional business says, "Study what's working for others," the Soulpreneur asks, *"What feels authentic to my unique gifts?"*

Where conventional business says "Scale bigger, faster," the Soulpreneur asks, *"What pace and size allows me to maintain presence and joy?"*

Where conventional business says "Push through resistance," the Soulpreneur asks, *"What is this resistance trying to teach me?"*

This isn't about rejecting smart business principles. It's about filtering them through your soul's wisdom rather than automatically adopting someone else's formula.

## LIVING THE SOULPRENEUR'S PATH

What does this look like in daily practice? It means:

- Making decisions from your center rather than from fear or pressure
- Designing offerings that energize rather than deplete you
- Marketing from authenticity rather than manipulation
- Setting boundaries that honor your energy and values
- Creating business models that support your desired lifestyle
- Measuring success by fulfillment as much as by finances
- Allowing intuition to guide your next steps

Most importantly, it means trusting that when you align with your soul purpose, you naturally attract the right opportunities, clients, and resources. Not through magical thinking, but because you're operating at a frequency that resonates with what's truly meant for you.

---

## ◎ TRY THIS REFLECTION: WALKING FORWARD AS A SOULPRENEUR

Let's anchor this moment with truth. In your journal, reflect on:

- What does soul alignment feel like in my body?
- What parts of me have softened, risen, or expanded on this journey?
- What do I now believe about success, leadership, and purpose?
- How will I show up differently as a Soulpreneur from this moment on?

## ONE FINAL WHISPER

You don't have to hustle your way to happiness.

You don't have to follow someone else's map.

You just have to choose to rise.

To be the woman who honours her soul.
To build from wholeness, not urgency.
To lead a life—and business—that feels like truth.

This is the Soulpreneur's Path.

**And it's already yours.**

# FINAL REFLECTION: YOU ARE READY

Do you remember the version of yourself who first picked up this book?

She may have felt burnt out, stuck in self-doubt, or uncertain of her path. She may have been juggling a hundred roles and silently asking herself, *"Is there more to life than this?"*

But she was also courageous. She was curious. She said yes to something deeper.

And here you are—having walked a journey most never dare to take. A journey inward.

Through these pages, you've explored your energy, confronted your patterns, reclaimed your voice, and reconnected with your truth. You've remembered that success isn't about striving or proving. It's about alignment. Integrity. Becoming.

You've begun to understand that your business is simply an extension of your frequency.

That who you are ***being*** matters more than what you are ***doing***.

That there's a version of you—free, whole, joyful, powerful—who is not waiting in the future but is already within you now.

This is the way of the Soulpreneur.

And this is just the beginning.

You don't need to wait to feel "ready."
You already are.

So, trust your inner compass.
Speak your truth with love.
Choose courage over comfort.
Let your energy lead.

Because when a woman chooses to rise in alignment with her soul, she doesn't just build a business.

She builds a legacy.

And perhaps most importantly, **she doesn't do it alone.**

# REFERENCES & CITATIONS

These works have inspired, informed, or been directly referenced throughout *Rewired To Rise*. They are included here to honour their contribution and offer further reading for the curious soulpreneur.

- Brown, B. (2012). *Daring greatly: How the courage to be vulnerable transforms the way we live, love, parent, and lead.* Gotham Books.
- Brown, B. (2018). *Dare to lead: Brave work. Tough conversations. Whole hearts.* Random House.
- Chödrön, P. (1996). *When things fall apart: Heart advice for difficult times.* Shambhala Publications. Goodreads+4Goodreads+4Google Books+4
- Chödrön, P. (2009). *Taking the leap: Freeing ourselves from old habits and fears.* Shambhala Publications.
- Csikszentmihalyi, M. (1990). *Flow: The psychology of optimal experience.* Harper & Row.
- Damasio, A. R. (1999). *The feeling of what happens: Body and emotion in the making of consciousness.* Harcourt Brace.
- Dispenza, J. (2013). *Breaking the Habit of Being Yourself: How to Lose Your Mind and Create a New One.* Hay House.

- Dispenza, J. (2017). *Becoming Supernatural: How Common People Are Doing the Uncommon.* Hay House.
- Feenstra, S., Begeny, C. T., Ryan, M. K., Rink, F., Stoker, J. I., & Jordan, J. (2020). *'impostor Syndrome' Holds Back Entrepreneurial Women.* ResearchGate.
- Fredrickson, B. L. (2001). The role of positive emotions in positive psychology: The broaden-and-build theory of positive emotions. *American Psychologist*, 56(3), 218–226. https://doi.org/10.1037/0003-066X.56.3.218
- Harvard Business Review. (2022, July). *The best leaders aren't afraid to be vulnerable.* https://hbr.org/2022/07/the-best-leaders-arent-afraid-of-being-vulnerable
- Hölzel, B. K., Carmody, J., Vangel, M., Congleton, C., Yerramsetti, S. M., Gard, T., & Lazar, S. W. (2011). Mindfulness practice leads to increases in regional brain gray matter density. *Psychiatry Research: Neuroimaging*, 191(1), 36–43. https://doi.org/10.1016/j.pscychresns.2010.08.006
- Jung, C. G. (1952). *Synchronicity: An Acausal Connecting Principle.* Princeton University Press.
- KPMG. (2020, October 8). *KPMG study finds 75% of female executives across industries have experienced impostor syndrome in their careers* [Press release]. PR Newswire. https://www.prnewswire.com/news-releases/kpmg-study-finds-75-of-female-executives-across-industries-have-experienced-imposter-syndrome-in-their-careers-301148023.html
- Lipton, B. H. (2015). *The Biology of Belief: Unleashing the Power of Consciousness, Matter & Miracles* (10th anniversary edition). Hay House.
- Hawkins, D. R. (1998). *Power vs. Force: The Hidden Determinants of Human Behavior.* Hay House.
- Hawkins, D. R. (2014). *Letting Go: The Pathway of Surrender.* Hay House.

- Singer, M. A. (2007). *The Untethered Soul: The Journey Beyond Yourself.* New Harbinger Publications.
- Singer, M. A. (2015). *The Surrender Experiment: My Journey Into Life's Perfection.* Hachette Books.
- Hölzel, B. K., et al. (2011). *Mindfulness practice leads to increases in regional brain gray matter density. Psychiatry Research: Neuroimaging, 191*(1), 36–43. https://doi.org/10.1016/j.pscychresns.2010.08.006
- HeartMath Institute. (2016). *Science of the Heart: Exploring the Role of the Heart in Human Performance.* https://www.heartmath.org/research/science-of-the-heart/details/
- Mangen, A., Walgermo, B. R., & Brønnick, K. (2013). *Reading linear texts on paper versus computer screen: Effects on reading comprehension.* International Journal of Educational Research, 58, 61–68. https://doi.org/10.1016/j.ijer.2012.12.002
- Morales, J. I. (2020). *The heart's electromagnetic field is your superpower. Psychology Today.* https://www.psychologytoday.com/au/blog/building-the-habit-of-hero/202011/the-hearts-electromagnetic-field-is-your-superpower
- Mueller, P. A., & Oppenheimer, D. M. (2014). *The pen is mightier than the keyboard: Advantages of longhand over laptop note taking.* Psychological Science, 25(6), 1159–1168. https://doi.org/10.1177/0956797614524581
- Pippa Campbell Health. (n.d.). *Why women should avoid cold water plunges.* Retrieved from https://www.pippacampbell-health.com/blog/cold-water-plunges/
- Premier Sport Psychology. (2025, February 21). *Cold plunging and intentional attention: Building resilience and focus in high-performance environments.* Retrieved from https://premiersportpsychology.com/2025/02/21/cold-plunging-and-intentional-attention-building-resilience-and-focus-in-high-performance-environments/

- ScienceDaily. (2025, March 28). *Cold plunges actually change your cells.* Retrieved from https://www.sciencedaily.com/releases/2025/03/250328173516.htm
- Sims, S. (2025). *ROAR, Revised Edition: Match Your Food and Fitness to Your Unique Female Physiology.* Rodale Books.
- VagusNerve.com. (n.d.). *The impact of cold water on the vagus nerve: A comprehensive analysis.* Retrieved from https://vagusnerve.com/the-impact-of-cold-water-on-the-vagus-nerve-a-comprehensive-analysis/

## HELP OTHERS BEGIN THEIR JOURNEY

Thank you for joining me on this transformational path through Rewired to Rise. Now that you've experienced the power of energetic alignment in your business, I have one final request:

*Would you share your experience with others?*

Your honest review could be the catalyst another entrepreneur needs to begin her own transformation. In just 2-3 minutes, you can create ripples that reach far beyond what you can see.

Many women are struggling with the same challenges you faced before reading this book:

- Burnout from constant hustle
- Disconnection from their authentic voice
- Uncertainty about their unique path
- Fear of standing in their full power

Your words might be exactly what they need to hear.

1. Scan the QR code
2. Share what resonated most deeply with you
3. Be honest about your experience—authenticity helps others most

Thank you for being part of this movement of women rising together—not through force, but through alignment with their truest selves.

With deep gratitude,

# ABOUT THE AUTHOR

Fiona Soutter's journey into the neuroscience of self-love and transformational leadership began unexpectedly after a life-altering car accident in 2014. While navigating chronic pain and recovery, Fiona realized that true healing required more than traditional methods—it demanded a profound understanding of the connection between mind, brain, energy, and lasting personal change.

Her quest led her deep into the study of quantum physics and neuroscience, guided by thought leaders such as Dr. Joe Dispenza and her personal mentor, Dr. Espen Wold-Jensen. Through this work, she learned how to break free from self-sabotaging patterns, rewire limiting beliefs, and step into her highest potential.

This transformation sparked not only personal breakthroughs but entrepreneurial success. In 2020, Fiona launched an e-commerce business that scaled to seven figures within 18 months—an achievement she attributes as much to inner work as to business strategy.

Today, Fiona brings together 20 years of teaching, coaching, and mentoring experience, entrepreneurial insight, and her passion for personal growth to empower others. Her writing makes complex concepts from neuroscience, quantum biology, and ancient wisdom accessible and practical.

Fiona is the author of *Rewiring Self-Love* and *Women Entrepreneurs Ready to Rise.*

Through her books, mentorship, and speaking, Fiona helps individuals break free from subconscious patterns, reconnect with their true selves, and create extraordinary lives—both personally and professionally.

Her mission is to bridge science and soul, offering tools and inspiration for those ready to rise beyond limitation and live their fullest potential.

Find out more about Fiona at https://fionasoutter.com

 facebook.com/likefionasoutter

# ALSO BY FIONA SOUTTER

## REWIRING SELF-LOVE: WHERE ANCIENT WISDOM MEETS NEUROSCIENCE

Are you ready to finally stop seeking validation outside yourself and build a deep, unshakable love from within?

In *Rewiring Self-Love*, Fiona Soutter combines the power of ancient wisdom with groundbreaking discoveries in neuroscience to help you release self-doubt, break free from old emotional patterns, and rewire your brain for lasting self-worth.

This isn't just another self-help book filled with theory — it's a practical, science-backed guide that walks you through exactly how to rebuild your relationship with yourself.

Inside, you'll discover:

➔ The neuroscience behind why self-love is essential for lasting change

➔ Tools and techniques that work with your brain's natural ability to rewire itself

➔ Guided practices to help you quiet your inner critic, set healthy boundaries, and build emotional resilience

➔ How to integrate small, powerful shifts into your daily life for transformation that lasts

Whether you struggle with people-pleasing, burnout, anxiety, or feeling like you're "never enough," *Rewiring Self-Love* offers a new path forward — one rooted in compassion, empowerment, and profound personal change.

*If you're ready to stop surviving and start thriving, this book will show you the way - Access the book here:* https://getbook.at/rewiringselflove

# READY TO TRANSFORM YOUR RELATIONSHIP WITH YOURSELF? JOIN THE 30-DAY SELF-LOVE CHALLENGE

If the ideas in this book have resonated with you, there's a way to turn them into daily practice—and experience even deeper shifts.

The 30-Day Self-Love Challenge gives you:

- **Daily guidance** that builds progressively to rewire your neural pathways
- **Simple practices** that take just 5-15 minutes each day
- **Scientific explanations** that connect each exercise to lasting change
- **Community support** from others on the same journey
- **Direct access** to my expertise throughout the challenge

This isn't about temporary feel-good moments. It's about creating sustainable change in how you treat yourself, speak to yourself, and show up in the world.

Many participants report significant shifts in their:

- Confidence and boundaries
- Emotional regulation
- Relationships with others
- Capacity for joy and presence
- Physical wellbeing

**Begin Your Practice**

Transform the insights from this book into embodied experience.

Simply scan the QR code to join the challenge and receive your first practice immediately.

Your journey to deeper self-love doesn't end with the final page of this book. It's just beginning.

With love and belief in your journey,

www.ingramcontent.com/pod-product-compliance
Lightning Source LLC
Chambersburg PA
CBHW052205090526
44583CB00017BA/2140